OLIVIER

THE COMPLETE CAREER   WITH 182 PHOTOGRAPHS

OLIVIER

Robert Tanitch

THAMES AND HUDSON

FOR JENNY AND PETER HANNA

Frontispiece: *Henry IV Part I*, 1945

Half-title illustrations
Prologue: *The Taming of the Shrew*, 1922
1920s: *Beau Geste*, 1929
1930s: *Romeo and Juliet*, 1935
1940s: *Richard III*, 1944
1950s: *Macbeth*, 1955
1960s: *Othello*, 1964
1970s: *Long Day's Journey Into Night*, 1972
1980s: *King Lear*, 1983

Printed in Spain by Artes Graficas Toledo S.A.

D.L. TO-501-1985

Contents

*Theatre 179 · Films 183 · Television 185
Director 186 · Management 187 · Radio 187
Awards and Honours 188*

With tributes from

Harry Andrews · Peggy Ashcroft · Michael Blakemore
Peter Brook · Constance Cummings · John Freebairn-Smith
Christopher Fry · John Gielgud · Katharine Hepburn · Jonathan Miller
John Mortimer · Denis Quilley · Dorothy Tutin

Introduction

Laurence Olivier is acknowledged, by the profession and the public alike, to be one of the great actors of the twentieth century. This book is a pictorial record and full chronology of his career in theatre, film, television and radio as actor, director, artistic director, producer and manager.

☆   ☆   ☆

If the greatness of an actor rests on the sheer number of great classical and modern roles he has played, and his success in them, then Laurence Olivier's greatness is unrivalled.

As a Shakespearian actor, he has triumphed in the one role in which most great actors have failed. He has been the blackest white actor in living memory. He has found new ways of playing a soldier-braggart, a Puritan and a Jew, which owe nothing to the stereotypes of the past. He has scored a personal success, single-handed, in what was thought to be an unplayable chamber of horrors. He has brought out a villain's latent homosexuality and found humour in an abdication scene, while his deaths at Antium (he has played the part twice) have been spectacular. Seven Shakespearian performances are preserved on film.

Outside of Shakespeare, he has been seen in Greek tragedy, Jacobean tragedy, Restoration comedy, eighteenth-century comedy, French farce and 1920s expressionism. He has appeared in four Shavian plays, one of them on film.

He has played a Swedish artillery captain, a Glaswegian Trotskyite, a Bulgarian buffoon, a Norwegian banker, a Norwegian architect, a Neapolitan hatter, a Carpathian Regent, a Russian conservationist, an American matinée idol and a Midlands salesman.

He has created roles for R.C. Sherriff, Noel Coward, J.B. Priestley, James Bridie, Terence Rattigan, Christopher Fry, John Osborne and Trevor Griffiths.

He has scored some notable doubles: alternating two roles with John Gielgud; contrasting a passionate warrior with a feeble justice of the peace; courting Cleopatra twice; and playing prelate and king in the same play.

He has also had a Viking's funeral, been groomed to be the leader of a neo-Fascist party and appeared in a nude show twice-nightly.

On the screen, both film and television, he has played a London bobby, an American tycoon, a Greek god, a Roman emperor, a Jewish cantor, a Muslim leader, a Dutch doctor, an Austrian minister, a Nazi and a Nazi-hunter. He has also been seen as a Russian doctor, a Russian diplomat, a Russian captain, a Russian engineer and a Russian premier.

He has acted within the law and outside of it as a solicitor, lawyer, barrister, detective, pickpocket, highwayman and spy.

He has played in adaptations of Emily Brontë, Jane Austen, Conan Doyle, Bram Stoker, Daphne du Maurier, Theodore Dreiser, Somerset Maugham, Graham Greene, Charles Dickens, Evelyn Waugh and John Fowles.

He has been seen as a journalist, a chauffeur, an alcoholic, a secondary-school teacher, a professional co-respondent, a novelist, a dress designer, two painters-in-exile and a balloonist.

He has served in the army, navy and air force, often in the highest rank. In addition to presiding over a notorious court martial, he has swashbuckled in Spain, murdered in New York, been murdered in Canada, courted an American chorus girl in London and married a transvestite in the country.

Olivier is first and foremost a *character* actor, equally adept in tragedy and comedy, capable of playing the most manly of kings, the most effeminate of fops – and sometimes on the same evening. In fact, it would seem that the only role he has not played is a rhinoceros. . . .

☆   ☆   ☆

Laurence Kerr Olivier was born in England, at Dorking in Surrey, on 22 May 1907, the son of a High Anglican clergyman. When the family moved to London three years later, he attended a number of preparatory schools before becoming, in 1916, one of the fourteen boarders of the choir school attached to All Saints Church, Margaret Street, W1. Here, under the guidance of the Precentor, Geoffrey Heald, he acted Shakespeare for the first time, playing Brutus, Maria and Katharine. Ellen Terry wrote in her diary: 'The small boy who played Brutus is already a great actor.' Olivier was ten years old.

In 1921, he went to St Edward's School, Oxford and stayed there for three years. In his final year, he appeared in the school production of *A Midsummer Night's Dream*. He wrote in his diary: 'Played Puck very well – much to everybody's disgust.'

In 1924, to his surprise, he found his father had decided on a career in the theatre for him. He auditioned for Elsie Fogerty, founder and principal of Central School of Speech Training and Dramatic Art, and won the scholarship and bursary he needed in order to be able to attend. In his diploma examination, the actress Athene Seyler bracketed him and Peggy Ashcroft with top marks for their performances in *The Merchant of Venice*.

While he was still at drama school, Olivier made his professional debut at Letchworth, as an assistant stage manager and Lennox in *Macbeth*. Once he had left Central, he walked-on, understudied and played small parts until he landed one of the juvenile leads in a touring production of *The Farmer's Wife*, which ended six months later in the Birmingham Repertory Theatre where Barry Jackson engaged him for a year.

At Birmingham, he played a wide variety of modern and classical parts, including Tony Lumpkin, Uncle Vanya and the rich son in *The Silver Box*. Perhaps his greatest personal success was in a modern-dress production of *All's Well That Ends Well*, in which his cowardly Parolles was a totally plausible braggart.

Two of the plays transferred to London: *Bird in Hand* in which he acted what he himself has described as 'the really moth-eaten juvenile' and *The Adding Machine* in which, with only the one scene as a ghost in a graveyard, St John Ervine singled him out for special praise, saying that he was the best actor in it.

At the Court Theatre, he also appeared in two more 'Shakespeare-in-plus-fours' productions: he was Malcolm in the disastrous *Macbeth* and a lord in the Induction scene in the far more successful *The Taming of the Shrew*. He created Martellus in Act V of Bernard Shaw's marathon *Back to Methuselah* and then, not yet twenty-one, he was cast in the leading role of the very first (and some thought the very last) performance of Alfred, Lord Tennyson's *Harold*. Once again, St John Ervine recognized his promise: 'He has the makings of a considerable actor in him.'

There were two decisions early in his career – one taken by him and one taken for him – which certainly affected his future. The first was when he chose not to transfer into the West End with *Journey's End*, preferring to play the lead in *Beau Geste*. Had he transferred with the play, he might then have gone with the director, James Whale, to Hollywood to make the 1931 *Frankenstein*. The second, a few years later, was when he was sacked from *Queen Christina*, in which he was cast as Greta Garbo's leading man. On both occasions he might well have become a movie star in America rather than a classical actor in England.

Beau Geste led to seven flops in a row and it wasn't until Noël Coward cast him in the cocktail-and-pyjama world of *Private Lives* that he had his first commercial success in London and New York.

In the early 1930s, he tended to specialize in such bad-tempered bravura parts as the American editor in *Biography*, philandering Bothwell in *Queen of Scots*, the athletic and temperamental film star in *Theatre Royal* and the wheelchair-bound sadist in *Ringmaster*. Always conscious of his audience, he played unashamedly to the gallery, never afraid to go over the top and give them the fireworks they had come to see. The end result was often highly mannered and highly strung, sometimes to the point of hysteria.

In 1935 John Gielgud invited him to alternate Romeo and Mercutio with him. Olivier has since said that what he was trying to achieve was poetic realism; only *The Observer* seems to have understood. His Romeo was dismissed, largely, one suspects, because he did not act or speak like Gielgud did; the contrast between classical and naturalistic acting jarred and he was accused of being a ranting, *prose* Romeo, lacking in poetry and tenderness. The critics preferred his Mercutio. However, what comes across forcibly in these reviews (which Olivier has admitted to having been deeply scarring) is the impetuosity, the passion and the vigour of his playing. James Agate, having pulled his performance to pieces, then added he had no hesitation in saying that Olivier was the most moving Romeo he had seen.

A major turning point was when Tyrone Guthrie invited him to lead the Old Vic Company in the 1937/1938 season, which firmly established him as a classical actor. The critics praised the sheer vitality and zest of his acting; time and time again, his physical energy, his vocal powers and his ability to set the stage alight were commented on. Having seen his Hamlet (in its entirety), Sir Toby Belch, Macbeth, Iago, Coriolanus and Vivaldi in James Bridie's *The King of Nowhere*, James Agate went even further and said that there was no doubt in his mind that the only signs of a great actor in the making in England was Laurence Olivier.

When the season ended, he went to America to make three films and while there he also appeared on Broadway: in the successful *No Time For Comedy* opposite

Katharine Cornell, and in the highly unsuccessful *Romeo and Juliet*, opposite Vivien Leigh, in which, playing to mocking laughter, they lost all their savings. He came back to England at the outbreak of the Second World War and served in the Fleet Air Arm.

In 1944 he became joint director of the Old Vic Company with Ralph Richardson and John Burrell and his acting of roles as varied as the Button-Moulder in *Peer Gynt*, Sergius in *Arms and the Man*, Richard III, Astrov in *Uncle Vanya*, Hotspur and Shallow in *Henry IV Parts I and II*, Oedipus, Puff in *The Critic* and King Lear established his pre-eminence in the profession. The season has passed into legend, and is also memorable for two dazzling transformations: first the virile, stammering Hotspur and the quavering, feeble Shallow; then the sullen godlike Oedipus and the foppish Puff. Oedipus' cry of agony, a cry worthy of Munch, is remembered to this day (even by people who never heard it). However, if there was one role more than any other which established Olivier's greatness, then that role must be his Richard III. Immensely popular with the public, the critics and theatre people, the performance is now part of twentieth-century theatrical consciousness and actors still walk in its huge shadow.

In 1948 he and Vivien Leigh led the Old Vic Company on a triumphant and gruelling ten-month tour of Australia and New Zealand in a repertoire which included *The Skin of Our Teeth*, *The School for Scandal* and *Richard III*. It was while he was in Sydney that he received a letter from Lord Esher, Chairman of the Old Vic governors, telling him that his five-year contract as director would not be renewed. (Ralph Richardson and John Burrell received similar letters.) This highly controversial decision proved to be not only a personal blow to Olivier but to the Old Vic itself.

Back in London, having taken his farewell of the company with Richard III, Sir Peter Teazle and the Chorus in Jean Anouilh's *Antigone*, he then became an actor-manager, acquiring the lease of the St James's Theatre and commissioning Christopher Fry to write a play for him. *Venus Observed*, an autumnal and mellow comedy, was followed by *Caesar and Cleopatra*, playing in tandem with *Antony and Cleopatra*, and was his contribution to the 1951 Festival of Britain. Two years later he appeared in Terence Rattigan's *The Sleeping Prince*, but it was not until 1955 at the Stratford Memorial Theatre that Olivier truly came into his own again.

The season began with his highly original and controversial Malvolio in *Twelfth Night*. Then came *Macbeth*. 'Last night Sir Laurence shook hands with greatness,' wrote Ken Tynan. 'I do not believe there is another actor in the world who can come near him,' wrote J.C. Trewin. For many people, critics and audiences, he was quite simply the best Macbeth since Macbeth. One landmark was immediately followed by another. The rarely performed *Titus Andronicus* was a most unexpected success: a revelation in fact, for there within the sensational and sickening horrors of melodrama he discovered the overwhelming pathos of tragedy.

The next major turning point in his career was when he invited John Osborne to write a play for him and appeared in *The Entertainer* at the Royal Court Theatre in 1957, the home of the English Stage Company and all the angry young men. Absurd as it may seem now, the very idea of Laurence Olivier appearing in such a role, in such a theatre, came as something of a shock to a public brought up on Laurence Olivier, the classical actor. However, his characteristic courage in risking his

◁ Archie Rice in *The Entertainer*, 1960

reputation to do something new paid off handsomely. Archie Rice, the fifth-rate music-hall comedian, proved to be one of his best parts and one of his most popular successes.

In 1959, he returned to Stratford to play Coriolanus whose arrogance, all sardonic smiles and studied romantic charm, had a magnificent, dynamic splendour. His next play, Ionesco's *Rhinoceros*, which did not repeat its continental critical success in England, was followed by Anouilh's *Becket* in New York in which he scored another notable double, playing both leading roles. Excellent twice over, he preferred the more emotional role of the king to the prelate; and certainly in its weeping, writhing anguish and its homosexual passion, it was the more showy part.

In 1961, at the invitation of its founder, Leslie Evershed Martin, he became the first director of the Chichester Festival Theatre, which opened the following year with *The Chances* and *The Broken Heart*, neither of which seemed worth reviving. The season was saved by a memorable *Uncle Vanya* in which he returned to one of his favourite roles – Astrov.

Back in London, in between the Chichester summer seasons, nobody, least of all himself, was pleased to see him as a balding, bespectacled Midlands salesman in *Semi-Detached*.

In 1962 he was appointed director of the National Theatre and in the next eleven years at the Old Vic, in addition to all his administrative duties, he played thirteen roles, including Astrov, Captain Brazen in *The Recruiting Officer*, Othello, Tattle in *Love for Love*, Edgar in *The Dance of Death*, Shylock, and James Tyrone in *Long Day's Journey Into Night*, all amongst his best work, equally impressive in their originality, wit, energy and technical skills. The Othello in particular, one of the great performances of our time, was a shattering theatrical experience, unlikely to be forgotten by anybody who saw it.

He also played Solness in *The Master Builder*, Chebutikin in *Three Sisters* and three scene-stealing cameos: the butler in *A Flea in Her Ear*, the solicitor in *Home and Beauty* and the grandfather in *Saturday, Sunday, Monday*.

Olivier naturally had hoped and intended to lead the company into the new theatre on the South Bank; but when the building, subject to innumerable delays, finally opened its doors to the public in 1974, he was no longer artistic director. He had already bowed out of the National playing an elderly Glaswegian Trotskyite in a controversial new play, *The Party*.

☆   ☆   ☆

Olivier's career in the cinema began in the early 1930s with a whole series of forgettable films in which, with his good looks and Ronald Colman moustache, he was cast as the romantic juvenile lead; by the end of the decade, in Hollywood, he had played Heathcliff in *Wuthering Heights*, Maxim de Winter in *Rebecca*, Darcy in *Pride and Prejudice*, and had become an international star.

On his return to England, he appeared in four propaganda films: the romantic *Lady Hamilton*, the realistic *49th Parallel*, the satirical *The Demi-Paradise* and the Shakespearian D-Day patriotic jingoism of *Henry V*.

His films since the war have been variable; his best performances have often been in supporting roles such as General Burgoyne in *The Devil's Disciple* or the cameos in *The Magic Box, The Battle of Britain,* and *Oh! What A Lovely War*.

Edgar in *The Dance of Death*, 1969 ▷

In the 1970s he brought off another of those remarkable doubles – first the brutal, powerful Nazi who gave Dustin Hoffman such an unforgettable lesson in dentistry in *Marathon Man*, and then the very elderly and very frail Jew in *The Boys from Brazil* – two characters so physically different that it was almost impossible to believe they were played by the same actor.

Though Olivier has appeared in over sixty films and has not appeared in the theatre for over ten years now, the public continues to think of him as a stage actor; partly, of course, because he *is* a stage actor and made his reputation in the classics, but also partly because so often when he is acting on the screen he does not seem to make any allowances for the medium. This was certainly true of the *Othello* film.

His reputation in the cinema rests on *Henry V, Hamlet* and *Richard III*. He will be remembered as the first director to bring Shakespeare successfully to the screen. *Henry V* was enormously popular with the critics and the public all over the world; and its release, coinciding as it did with that legendary first season at the Old Vic at the end of the Second World War, reaffirmed his position as the leader of his profession. It is fortunate that *Richard III*, an excellent record of how Shakespeare used to be acted, should preserve so well for posterity his most famous stage performance; but it is *Hamlet*, stunningly photographed in black and white, which is the best *film*.

☆   ☆   ☆

Olivier has directed a wide range of classics, including plays by Shakespeare, Sheridan, Thornton Wilder, Anouilh, Christopher Fry, Sean O'Casey, Giraudoux and J.B. Priestley.

His all-star revival of *Uncle Vanya*, instantly recognized as one of the great Chekhovian productions of our time, put the Chichester Festival Theatre firmly on the map. The greatness lay in the fine ensemble playing of the highly distinguished cast who, most movingly, caught the tragedy of unfulfilled lives.

There were also three notable productions at the National Theatre. *The Crucible* emerged unmistakably as a modern classic, scotching the absurd idea that since McCarthyism was dead, Arthur Miller no longer had anything to say to an audience. Chekhov's bitter tirade against life's injustices in *Three Sisters* became a sad lament for lost youth, its opportunities denied, its chances missed, and a great hymn to the human spirit; while *Love's Labour's Lost*, drawing on Walter Pater's idea of 'an ancient tapestry' put the romantic excesses and pedantic affectations back to the fifteenth century and the badinage was acted with almost balletic artifice.

☆   ☆   ☆

Though Olivier had, in fact, made his first television appearance as early as 1937 in excerpts from *Macbeth*, he waited another twenty-one years before making his official debut in *John Gabriel Borkman*, which proved to be a singularly unpopular choice with the general public.

He made his American debut in 1959 in *The Moon and Sixpence*, playing a painter-in-exile, a Gauguin-like part he much enjoyed and which won him his first Emmy. Two years later he was cast as the whiskey-priest in *The Power and the Glory*, a role he had coveted ever since seeing Paul Scofield play it on the London stage. Thirteen years later he acted with Katharine Hepburn for the first time and

◁ *Hamlet, 1948*

they both won an Emmy for their performances in *Love Among the Ruins*. In the interim he made some commercials for Polaroid, but only on the strictest understanding that they would not be shown in the UK.

On English television, apart from doing the prologue to *Theatre Royal*, the 1967 all-star benefit in aid of the Florence Disaster Fund, he was not seen until 1976 when he produced and acted in the Granada series, *The Best Play of –*. The season included *Cat on a Hot Tin Roof*, *Come Back, Little Sheba*, *Daphne Laureola* and *Saturday, Sunday, Monday*. He also directed *Hindle Wakes*. For many he was at his best in *The Collection* with the enigmatic elegance of Harold Pinter, playing the homosexual dress designer.

In the 1980s he has appeared in three notable productions: as Lord Marchmain in *Brideshead Revisited*, as the blind barrister in *A Voyage Round My Father* and as the painter in *The Ebony Tower*. He also has appeared in Shakespeare, returning to a role he had not played for well over thirty years. The television producers described *King Lear* as a play about 'the courage of a man of seventy-five playing such a difficult role after a long illness' and his performance won him his sixth Emmy in 1984.

☆　　　☆　　　☆

As a theatrical manager, Olivier has not always been lucky, either financially or critically, but thanks to him London has been able to see Vivien Leigh in Tennessee Williams' *A Streetcar Named Desire*, Orson Welles in *Othello*, Gian Carlo Menotti's opera *The Consul*, Ray Lawler's *Summer of the Seventeenth Doll* with the Australian cast, and the first performance of Beverley Cross' *One More River*.

As the artistic director of the Old Vic, the Chichester Festival Theatre and the National Theatre, he has been responsible, directly and indirectly, for some of the most outstanding productions and performances of our time. At the National, under a general policy of 'the best of everything', a wide repertoire of familiar and unfamiliar classics, plus new plays by Peter Shaffer, Tom Stoppard, Charles Wood, Peter Nichols and Trevor Griffiths were produced. Everything, it might be said, from Arrabal to Zuckmayer.

☆　　　☆　　　☆

At the start of his career, Olivier could have been a glamorous movie star, a matinée idol or a classical actor; he opted to be the last and managed to be all three. The ensuing photographs confirm not only the sheer variety of roles he has played but his extraordinary and seemingly endless ability to change himself physically with each part. He is, by common consent, one of the greatest actors of our time, whose performances, in their magnetism, dynamism, stamina and technical resources, have always aroused the keenest interest, the fiercest controversy and the greatest excitement in audiences and actors alike.

This book, both a record and a tribute, celebrates a career which, in its contribution to twentieth-century theatre and theatrical consciousness, has been incalculable.

Prologue

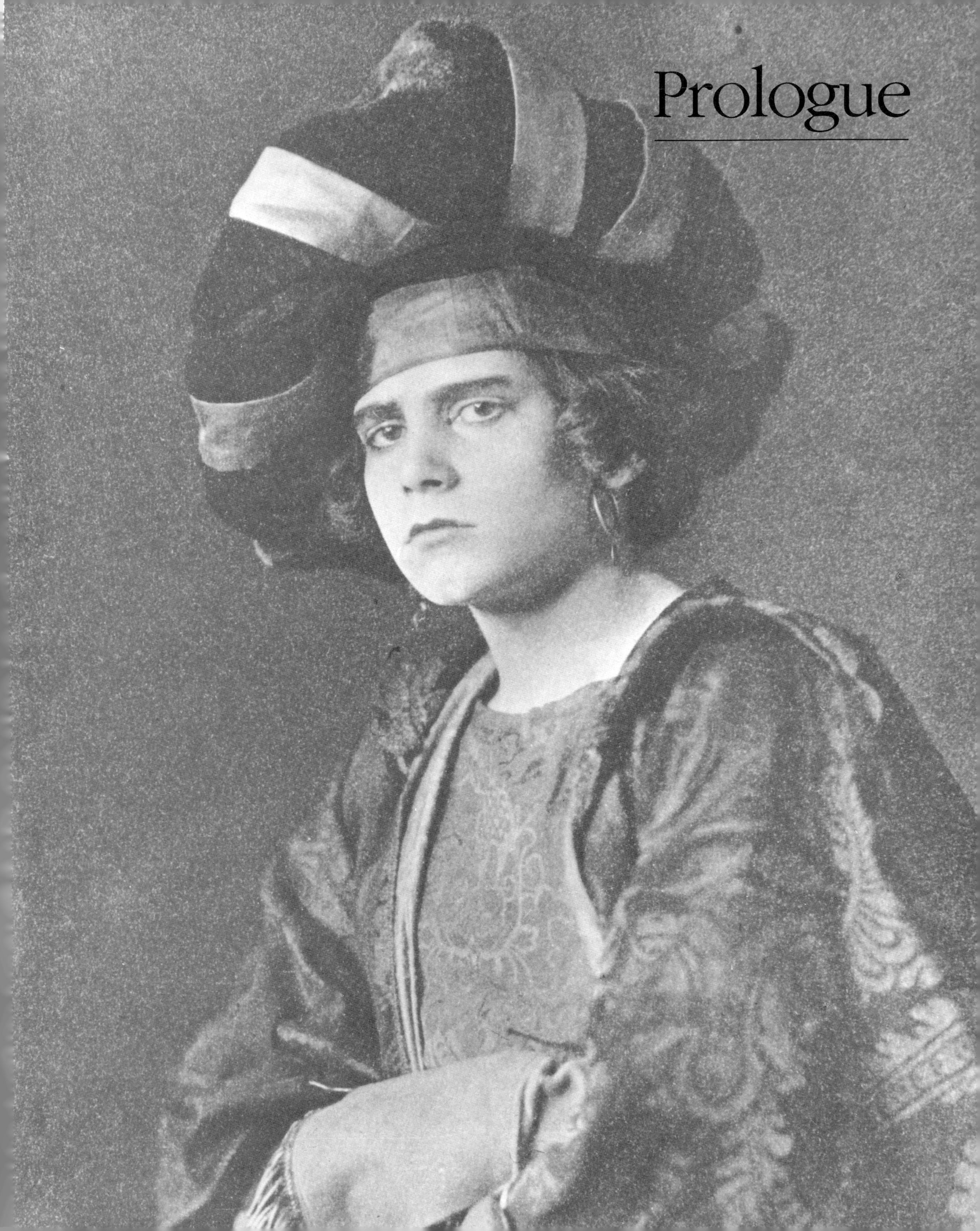

1 *Twelfth Night 1917*

Laurence Olivier as Maria, Fabia Drake as Sir Toby Belch, John Freebairn-Smith as Feste, Jack Sutters as Malvolio and Fred Oxley as Sir Andrew Aguecheek in Shakespeare's *Twelfth Night*, directed by Geoffrey Heald at All Saints choir school.

My recollections of Larry's actual performances as a boy are naturally a bit hazy after all this time. Anything he did was always well above boys' standards but while I feel his portrayal of Maria was very good without anything startling, I really think his Brutus was amazingly mature and very moving. Later of course his Katherina was equally brilliant in quite another way and was seen by hundreds in the Memorial Theatre at Stratford. Whilst at school in

Margaret Street we others used to look forward to Saturday evenings when Larry would entertain us with impromptu impersonations (e.g. eccentric members of the staff such as the organist, and of the kitchen staff who served the choristers at table, film actors such as Chaplin, Fatty Arbuckle, Keystone Cops, etc.), home-made sketches in company with two or three other choristers, mostly mimed but sometimes with words. Saturday and Sunday were the only two days without evening school and prep, so, as you can imagine, we always had great fun on Saturday evenings in an era when all of us were used to entertaining ourselves – no TV, not even radio. By the time radio arrived we had all left the choir school!

John Freebairn-Smith

2 *The Taming of the Shrew* 1922

Geoffrey Heald as Petruchio and Laurence Olivier as Katharine in
Shakespeare's *The Taming of the Shrew*, directed by Geoffrey Heald
at the Memorial Theatre, Stratford-upon-Avon.

On 28 April 1922, the Precentor and choristers of All Saints
Church made a pilgrimage to Stratford-upon-Avon to honour the
memory of Shakespeare. In the morning, robed and carrying lighted
tapers, they laid a wreath and sang at the poet's grave. In the
afternoon, at the invitation of the governors of the Memorial Theatre,
they performed *The Taming of the Shrew*, which was highly praised.
Olivier was fourteen years old.

*Some of the acting was really admirable. The Shrew was boldly and
vigorously played, with dark, flashing eyes and a spiteful voice.*
Birmingham Post

*The Katherina was an excellent study of scowling bad temper. The
lad's delivery of the tamed shrew's closing oration was a capital
effort.*

Birmingham Mail

*The boy who took the part of Kate made a fine, bold, black-eyed
hussy, badly in need of taming, and I cannot remember any actress
in the part who looked better.*

The Daily Telegraph

3,4 *A Midsummer Night's Dream 1923*

Laurence Olivier and the hall of St Edward's School, Oxford. He
played Puck in Shakespeare's *A Midsummer Night's Dream*, a school
production directed by W.H.A. Cowell.

   The sixteen-year-old Olivier, dancing up and down the aisles, his
face lit by two torch lamps fixed to a harness round his chest, scored
an unexpected success with his schoolfellows.

5 *The Farmer's Wife 1926*

Laurence Olivier and Freda Clark in Eden Philpott's *The Farmer's Wife*, directed by H.K. Ayliff.

Olivier played the love-sick country bumpkin, Richard Coaker, in this touring production which finally arrived at the Birmingham Repertory Theatre where he joined Barry Jackson's famous company for a year.

6 *The Well of the Saints 1927*

Laurence Olivier (second from left) as Mat Simon in J.M. Synge's *The Well of the Saints*, directed by W.G. Fay at the Birmingham Repertory Theatre.

7 *The Third Finger 1927*

Charles Cullum, Elana Aherne, Melville Cooper, Jane Welsh, Laurence Olivier and Dorothy Turner in R.R. Whittaker's *The Third Finger*, directed by W.G. Fay at the Birmingham Repertory Theatre.

Olivier played one of the young men who is taken in completely when the village schoolmistress pretends she has got married during a holiday in London.

8 *The Mannoch Family 1927*

Jane Welsh, Melville Cooper and Laurence Olivier in Murray McClymond's *The Mannoch Family*, directed by W.G. Fay at the Birmingham Repertory Theatre.

Olivier played a well-to-do young man, who falls in love with the daughter of a drunken, brutal poultry farmer.

9 *Uncle Vanya 1927*

Laurence Olivier as Vanya in Anton Chekhov's *Uncle Vanya*, directed by W.G. Fay at the Birmingham Repertory Theatre.

10 *All's Well That Ends Well 1927*

Laurence Olivier (on the ground) as Parolles in a modern-dress production of Shakespeare's *All's Well That Ends Well,* directed by W.G. Fay at the Birmingham Repertory Theatre.

Taking as one of his clues to Parolles' character the line to the effect that 'the soul of the man is in his clothes', Olivier presented a well-dressed, good-looking First World War officer who was a totally plausible braggart.

It was clearly a pity that this particular revival in a whole series of 'Shakespeare-in-plus-fours' productions, so much favoured by Barry Jackson, was not seen in London instead of the disastrous *Macbeth* in which Olivier was to play Malcolm at the Court Theatre in 1928.

12 *Bird in Hand* 1927

Percy Rhodes, Carrie Baillie, Frank Randall, Charles Maunsell, Ivor Barnard, Laurence Olivier and Peggy Ashcroft in John Drinkwater's *Bird in Hand*, directed by the author at the Birmingham Repertory Theatre.

When the play transferred to the Royalty Theatre, London, in 1928, Olivier repeated his role of the squire's son who wants to marry the village innkeeper's daughter, but finds her father does not believe girls should marry above their station.

Miss Peggy Ashcroft's Joan Greenleaf was a charming, sensible, straightforward impersonation. The part, naturally drawn, was naturally acted. Mr. Laurence Olivier as Gerry Arnwood gave a companion portrait. Only one moment was out of character, and that his sentimental kissing the door of his sweetheart's room.

Birmingham Post

11 *She Stoops to Conquer* 1927

Laurence Olivier as Tony Lumpkin in Oliver Goldsmith's *She Stoops to Conquer*, directed by W.G. Fay at the Birmingham Repertory Theatre.

Praise is due to Mr. Laurence Olivier for his Tony Lumpkin. There is a happy avoidance of the tendency all too apparent as a rule to transform the young squire into a mere uncouth clown.

Birmingham Mail

13 *Advertising April 1927*

Laurence Olivier and Dorothy Turner in Herbert Farjeon and Horace Horsnell's *Advertising April*, directed by W.G. Fay at the Birmingham Repertory Theatre.

Olivier played a romantic poet, who is in love with a movie star and would like her to be less artificial.

The company was criticized for spoiling a charming play by vulgarizing the comedy and turning it into a bad farce.

Indeed, of the four major personages the only player who was genuinely in character was Mr. Laurence Olivier as Mervyn Jones, though even he was given some pieces of farcical 'business' which were not merely unnecessary, but disturbing.

Birmingham Post

14 *The Silver Box 1927*

Laurence Olivier and Robert Lang in John Galsworthy's *The Silver Box*, directed by W.G. Fay at the Birmingham Repertory Theatre.

Olivier played the rich Liberal MP's dissolute son, who steals a prostitute's purse and gets off scot free, while the poor char's out-of-work husband, who steals a cigarette box, goes to prison.

At the moment, when police action is being criticised and while unemployment remains a vital problem of our social system, the Repertory revival is peculiarly opportune, and consequently the demerits of one law for the well-to-do and another for the poor are hammered home with added force.

Birmingham Gazette.

15 *The Adding Machine 1927*

Barbara Horder and Laurence Olivier in the graveyard scene in Elmer Rice's expressionistic fable, *The Adding Machine*, a satire on modern civilization, directed by W.G. Fay at the Birmingham Repertory Theatre. The play transferred to the Court Theatre, London, in 1928.

Olivier played the ghost of a young man who has murdered his mother. St John Ervine, the Irish dramatist and critic, singled out his performance as the best ('He had little to do, but he acted.') and he was also praised by the other London critics as the only actor to get the American accent right.

16 *Aren't Women Wonderful?* 1927

Dorothy Turner and Laurence Olivier in Harris Dean's *Aren't Women Wonderful?*, directed by W.G. Fay at the Birmingham Repertory Theatre.

Olivier played the unstable, ambitious engineer, recently married, who is being seduced by the wife of the man who is financing the motor engine he has invented.

Mr. Laurence Olivier . . . achieved a real success in his exceptionally difficult task of interpreting the weak and in many respects very unsympathetic character of Ben Hawley.

Birmingham Mail

17 *The Road to Ruin* 1927

Laurence Olivier, Frank Randall, Gerald Lee and Percy Rhodes in Thomas Holcroft's *The Road to Ruin*, directed by W.G. Fay at the Birmingham Repertory Theatre. Olivier played Mr Milford.

18 *Macbeth 1928*

Nigel Clarke as Ross, Scott Sunderland as Macduff and Laurence Olivier as Malcolm in the modern-dress production of Shakespeare's *Macbeth*, directed by H.K. Ayliff at the Court Theatre.

19 *The Taming of the Shrew 1928*

Laurence Olivier as a lord, Charles Lamb as a page in drag and Frank Pettingell as Christopher Sly in a modern-dress production of Shakespeare's *The Taming of the Shrew*, directed by H.K. Ayliff at the Court Theatre.

Once the Induction scene was finished, all Olivier had to do was sit in the stage box in full view of the audience until the play was over. According to his autobiography, he whiled away the time trying to 'corpse' Ralph Richardson, who was playing Tranio.

20 *Beau Geste 1929*

Edmund Willard, Jack Hawkins, Robert Irvine and Laurence Olivier in Basil Dean and Charlton Mann's adaptation of P.C. Wren's *Beau Geste*, directed by Basil Dean at His Majesty's.

Olivier played Beau, seen here being given a 'Viking's Funeral' at Fort Zinderneuf by his two brothers.

Olivier has admitted to using the two performances of R.C. Sherriff's *Journey's End* by the Stage Society (in which he created the role of Captain Stanhope) as a sort of audition piece for Basil Dean, who was casting *Beau Geste*. He landed the lead and seven flops followed in quick succession.

The critics dismissed the play as fifth-form entertainment and Dean's technically stunning but interminable production (which on the first night did not finish till 11.45 p.m.) as beautiful spectacle and nothing else.

21 *The Circle of Chalk 1929*

Laurence Olivier in Klabund's *The Circle of Chalk*, picturesque Chinoiserie directed by Basil Dean at the New Theatre.

Olivier played the young prince who rescues a tea-house girl, wrongfully accused of murder, from death. Anna May Wong, the little Chinese film star with the disconcertingly big American accent, won praise for her movement and silences. Olivier, suffering from laryngitis, had to sing a solo. The play was not a particularly happy experience.

22 *The Stranger Within* 1929

Roland Culver, Reginald Bach, Annie Esmond, Laurence Olivier and Olga Lindo in Crane Wilbur's *The Stranger Within*, directed by Reginald Bach at the Garrick Theatre.

A chorus girl with a heart of gold steps out of the wrecked Canadian Pacific Express and into the lives of three brothers on a farm in the Middle West. Olivier, who as James Agate said, 'gets out of bad parts all the charm there is in them', played the younger brother who marries her. She is later accused of murdering their baby.

Most critics thought the best thing about the play was the offstage sound effects of the crashing train.

23 *Murder on the Second Floor* 1929

Laurence Olivier and Phyllis Konstam in Frank Vosper's *Murder on the Second Floor*, directed by William Mollison at the Eltinge Theatre, New York.

This play within a play did not repeat its London success and was off within five weeks. Olivier, making his Broadway debut, was cast as the young author who turns the guests in his mother's boarding house into characters in his detective melodrama.

24 *The Last Enemy* *1929*

Marjorie Mars and Laurence Olivier in Frank Harvey's *The Last Enemy*, directed by Tom Walls at the Fortune Theatre.

Olivier played a shell-shocked Royal Flying Corps officer on fourteen days' leave in wartime London. The play, a mixture of mushy sentiment and allegorical solemnity, which opened and closed on a stairway to paradise, established him as a leading juvenile. He considered it a fine play and a brilliantly effective part; but it did not break his run of bad luck. The public clearly thought it too gloomy an entertainment for Christmas and stayed away.

25 *The Temporary Widow* 1930

Felix Aylmer and Laurence Olivier in the English-language version of
The Temporary Widow, a film directed by Gustav Ucicky. There was
also a German-language version.

   Olivier played an artist who is presumed to have been drowned
by his wife. Based on Curt Goetz's courtroom drama, *Hokuspokus*, it
was Olivier's first film, apart from one day's work as an extra in 1925.

26 *Too Many Crooks* 1930

Laurence Olivier and Dorothy Boyd in *Too Many Crooks*, a film
directed by George King.

   Olivier was cast as a playboy, who is seen here being caught
burgling his own house by a policewoman in civilian clothes.

27 *Private Lives 1930*

Laurence Olivier and Noël Coward in the cocktail-and-pyjama world of *Private Lives*, that verbal and physical sparring match Noël Coward had written for himself and Gertrude Lawrence, directed by the author at the Phoenix Theatre in 1930. The play transferred to Times Square, New York, in 1931.

Olivier played the priggish husband whose wife elopes with her first husband while they are on their honeymoon.

28 *Private Lives 1930*

Laurence Olivier and Adrienne Allen in *Private Lives*.

The comedy, all brittle staccato rudeness and incessant trivial flippancy, is dangerously thin; but this has never interfered with its success. As his preface to the play confirms, Coward was only too well aware what unrewarding roles the supporting parts are:

As a complete play, it leaves a lot to be desired, principally owing to my dastardly and conscienceless behaviour toward Sybil and Victor, the secondary characters. These, poor things, are little better than ninepins, lightly wooden, and only there at all to be repeatedly knocked down and stood up again.

He therefore cast two attractive personalities in the roles to explain why the jaggedly sophisticated Amanda and Elyot would ever have given them a second thought, let alone marry them.

29 *Potiphar's Wife   1931*

Laurence Olivier and Nora Swinburne in *Potiphar's Wife*, a film directed by Maurice Elvery. The US title is *Her Strange Desire*.

Olivier played a chauffeur whose employer, the wife of an English lord, takes him to court accusing him of having assaulted her; the truth is she has failed to seduce him.

30 *Westward Passage   1932*

Laurence Olivier and Ann Harding in *Westward Passage*, a film directed by Robert Milton.

Olivier played a jealous and temperamental writer, who marries, divorces and remarries the same woman.

31 *Perfect Understanding 1933*

Laurence Olivier, Gloria Swanson and Nigel Playfair in *Perfect Understanding*, a film directed by Cyril Gardner.

Olivier played the husband who confesses to an affair and finds his wife unexpectedly jealous.

Gloria Swanson invited Olivier ('his good looks were positively blinding') to be, on her own admission, her somewhat *young* leading man in her first British film. *Perfect Understanding* was 'a misnomer if ever there was one', said Olivier; 'a disaster,' agreed Miss Swanson, who lost a lot of money.

32 *No Funny Business* 1933

Laurence Olivier and Jill Esmond as two professional co-respondents who mistake each other for clients in *No Funny Business*, a film directed by John Stafford and Victor Hanbury. The US title is *The Professional Co-respondents*.

33 *The Rats of Norway* 1933

Helen Spencer, Raymond Massey and Laurence Olivier in Keith Winter's *The Rats of Norway*, directed by Raymond Massey at the Playhouse Theatre.

The lemmings of the title are the staff of a Northumbrian preparatory school. Olivier played the decent sports master who falls in love with the self-destructive French mistress. His performance, vividly remembered by Harold Hobson, theatre critic for *The Sunday Times*, and used by him as a touchstone all his life, was admired for its strength and sincerity, though criticized for its inaudibility.

Olivier left the cast to go to Hollywood to be Greta Garbo's leading man in *Queen Christina*, only to find that she preferred John Gilbert, and he was fired.

34 *The Green Bay Tree 1933*

Laurence Olivier and James Dale in Mordaunt Shairp's *The Green Bay Tree*, directed by Jed Harris at the Cort Theatre, New York.

Olivier played a young man who is adopted by a rich homosexual and introduced to a life of luxury.

In the horrifying scene where he is beaten into slavish submission by his benefactor's abnormal attraction for him, his acting becomes not acting, but an exhibition of emotional collapse so painful to witness that the eyes of the audience are torn away; the spectacle of his ignominy actually becomes too terrible to bear.

Florence Fisher Parry *Pittsburgh Press*

35 *Biography 1934*

Ina Claire, Joan Wyndham and Laurence Olivier in S.N. Behrman's *Biography*, directed by Noël Coward at the Globe Theatre.

Olivier played the rude and intolerant editor of a popular American magazine who wants to publish a portrait painter's memoirs – memoirs which will jeopardize a senator's career. James Agate wrote: 'I foresee that his continuous ill-temper will make him a matinée star for masochists.'

The play, despite the presence of the American star, Ina Claire, returning to London after twenty years, failed to repeat its Broadway success. Olivier, in *Confessions of an Actor*, blamed Noël Coward's direction.

36 *Queen of Scots 1934*

Gwen Ffrangcon-Davies as Mary, Margaret Webster as Mary Beaton, Laurence Olivier as Bothwell and Glen Byam Shaw as Darnley in Gordon Daviot's *Queen of Scots*, directed by John Gielgud at the New Theatre.

Ralph Richardson was originally cast as Bothwell but withdrew after only one rehearsal, unhappy with the romantic scenes, and Olivier took over the role. The critics admired his handsome bad-tempered virility and praised his splendid ferocity and dash, though some thought him more Hollywood than Holyrood:

I did not like Mr Laurence Olivier's Bothwell, for I don't believe that any sixteenth century Scottish noble could have so many of the attributes and mannerisms of Mr. Clark Gable.

Evening News

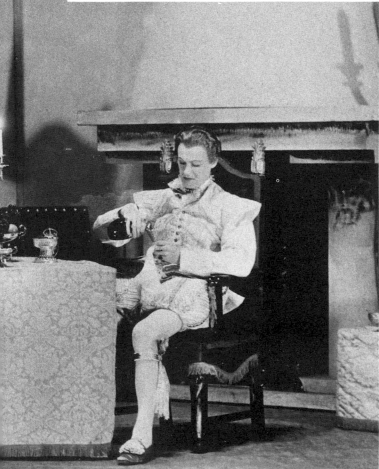

37 *Theatre Royal* 1934

George Zucco, Laurence Olivier, Madge Titheradge, Marie Tempest, Margaret Vines, Mary Merrall and W. Graham-Browne in Edna Ferber and George S. Kaufman's *Theatre Royal*, directed by Noël Coward at the Lyric Theatre.

The play is a joke at the expense of America's most famous theatrical family. Olivier was cast in the John Barrymore role and, one night, playing the exuberant and flamboyant character very much in the heroic and athletic Douglas Fairbanks manner, he vaulted over the banister rail, slipped as he landed and fractured two ankle bones. In his next play, having fully recovered, he found himself spending the whole evening in a wheelchair.

38 *Ringmaster* 1935

Cathleen Nesbitt, Colin Keith-Johnston, Dame May Witty, Dorothy Hyson, Nigel Patrick, Laurence Olivier and Jill Esmond in Keith Winter's *Ringmaster*, directed by Raymond Massey at the Shaftesbury Theatre.

Olivier played a crippled sadist, a former matinée idol, who runs a Devonshire guest house and wrecks the lives of the people staying there.

Mr. Laurence Olivier, as the dark, ferocious Hammond, continually lit up his part with baleful flashes, and easily had the house cheering with his ultimate contortions on the floor. But I wished he would not clip his speech, and throw away the last words of a sentence; it was a continual strain to hear him.

Ivor Brown *The Observer*

39 *Golden Arrow 1935*

Greer Garson, Cecil Parker and Laurence Olivier in Sylvia Thompson and Victor Cunard's *Golden Arrow*, directed by Laurence Olivier at the Whitehall Theatre.

Olivier played a rising politician who refuses to take his mistress with him when he has to attend a conference abroad.

The play marked the debut of Greer Garson on the London stage and Olivier's first steps into theatrical management. It was not a success. *The Times* said the politician had nothing to recommend him except that he was played by Olivier; while James Agate commented: 'Throughout the evening Mr. Olivier had not one single word which was worth speaking or hearing.'

Keith Winter has not written a good play. On the other hand he has given Laurence Olivier such an effective piece of bravura acting to do that people may flock to the theatre to see it. No actor could have asked a better chance for fireworks. No actor could have produced better pyrotechnics than Mr. Olivier.

W.A. Darlington *The Daily Telegraph*

40 *Romeo and Juliet 1935*

Laurence Olivier as Romeo, Edith Evans as the Nurse and John Gielgud as Mercutio in Shakespeare's *Romeo and Juliet*, directed by John Gielgud at the New Theatre.

I believe that my attitude, passion, poetic-realism and Italianate silhouette were all aimed in the right direction.

Laurence Olivier

Mr. Laurence Olivier can play many parts. Romeo is not one of them. His voice has neither the tone nor the compass and his blank verse is the blankest I have ever heard. When Miss Ashcroft asked him, 'Wherefore art thou, Romeo?' I was inclined to echo the question.

Stephen Williams *Evening Standard*

He is a ranting, writhing Romeo, whose words are often roared too loudly to be clearly heard, and he has no tenderness which is an even more serious fault. Mr. Laurence Olivier is temperamentally ill at ease with Romeo. He shows us none of those marvellous quick accelerations of which an actor must be capable who plays a part that seems to have been written in sudden flashes of illumination.

The Times

He has not the lyrical quality either of voice or manner. He seems bewildered, disinterested at first, almost scornful of what he has to say, and needlessly violent later on. But his vigour and passion are welcome in their own way.

Manchester Post

41 *Romeo and Juliet 1935*

Peggy Ashcroft as Juliet and Laurence Olivier as Romeo in Shakespeare's *Romeo and Juliet*.

The Romeo of Laurence Olivier certainly gave us gallant bearing, the hot outpouring of words, and the impetuous haste, and in the cell scene this virile actor displayed a 'fine classical phrensy'. But Mr. Olivier's voice is resonant rather than melodious enough for Shakespeare's tenderest verse.

A.E. Wilson *Evening Star*

I have seen few sights so moving as the spectacle of Mr. Olivier's Romeo, stunned with Juliet's beauty, fumbling for words with which to say his love. . . . I am not bold enough to say what Shakespeare would or would not have liked, but I think his eyes would have shone had he seen this Romeo: young and ardent and full of clumsy grace.

The Observer

Mr. Olivier's Romeo suffered enormously from the fact that the spoken poetry of the part eluded him. In his delivery he brought off a twofold inexpertness which approached virtuosity – that of gabbling all the words in a line and uttering each line as a staccato whole cut off from its fellows.

James Agate *The Sunday Times*

I was trying to sell realism in Shakespeare – I believed in it with my whole soul.

Laurence Olivier

So much has been written about Larry – his genius, his courage – all he has done for our theatre. What is there left to say? How fortunate one is to have had his friendship since student days, sixty years ago; to have played Juliet to his definitive Romeo; and seen him become the Titan of the English Theatre.

Peggy Ashcroft

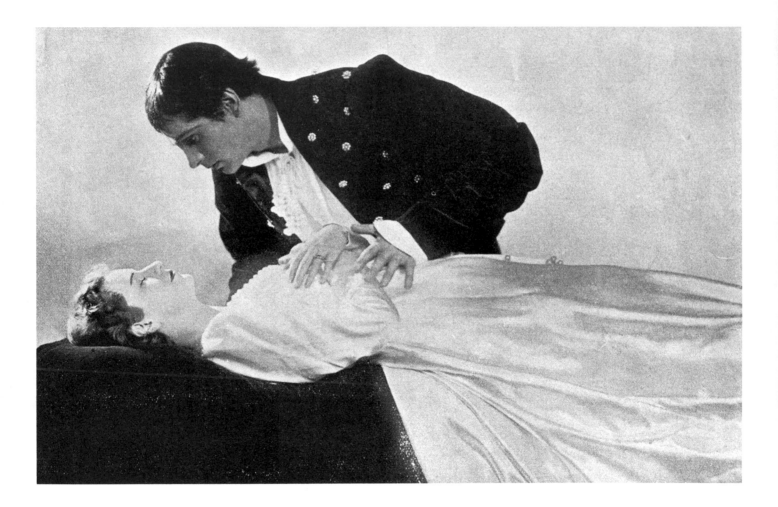

42 *Romeo and Juliet 1935*

Peggy Ashcroft as Juliet and Laurence Olivier as Romeo in Shakespeare's *Romeo and Juliet*, directed by John Gielgud at the New Theatre.

43 *Romeo and Juliet 1935*

John Gielgud as Romeo and Laurence Olivier as Mercutio in Shakespeare's *Romeo and Juliet*.

Mr. Olivier's Mercutio has a splendid dash and swagger; never was a man so nearly mad and so well pleased with himself, intoxicated with the light and heady wines of genius.

The Times

This is a brilliant piece of work – full of zest, humour and virility.
W.A. Darlington The Daily Telegraph

His Mercutio is a grand example of bravura. Gaiety, whimsicality and ferocity are fused into one mood.

Daily Mail

Mr. Olivier gave us a Mercutio whose every word struck fire, whose rattling oaths and wanton fantasies shocked and delighted, and whose death had a terrible and eternal significance, because it was the death of all youth.

Evening Standard

There is plenty of honest rock about Mr. Olivier's Mercutio, though he turns on the poetry in the way that athletic young fellows turn on the morning bath.

James Agate The Sunday Times

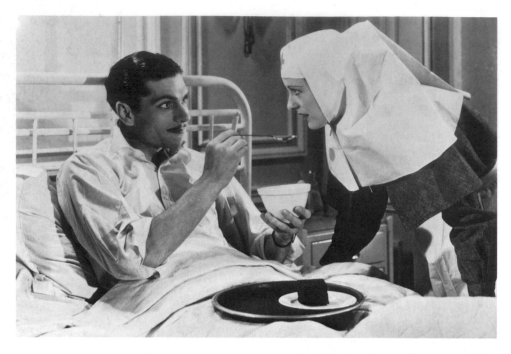

44 *Moscow Nights* 1935

Laurence Olivier and Penelope Dudley Ward in *Moscow Nights*, a film directed by Anthony Asquith. Olivier played a young Russian captain who is about to be shot for being a spy. The US title is *I Stand Condemned*.

45 *Bees on the Boatdeck* 1936

Rene Ray and Laurence Olivier in J.B. Priestley's farcical tragedy, *Bees on the Boatdeck*, a political satire, directed by Laurence Olivier and Ralph Richardson at the Lyric Theatre.

Olivier played an officer on the tramp steamer, SS *Gloriana*, which everybody is trying to blow up.

46 *Conquest of the Air* *1936*

Laurence Olivier as Vincent Lunardi, the first balloonist to fly over London in 1784, in *Conquest of the Air*, a history of aviation, directed by Alexander Shaw, John Monk Saunders, Alexander Esway and Zoltan Korda.

47 *Hamlet 1937*

Laurence Olivier as Hamlet and Dorothy Dix as Gertrude in Shakespeare's *Hamlet*, directed by Tyrone Guthrie at the Old Vic Theatre.

48 *Hamlet 1937*

Laurence Olivier in Shakespeare's *Hamlet*.

As a result of seeing his Romeo and Mercutio, Guthrie invited Olivier to lead the Old Vic Company in the 1937/1938 season and the opening play was *Hamlet* in its entirety. Both director and actor were influenced by Dr Ernest Jones, President of the International Psycho-Analytical Association. He saw the hero as having an Oedipus complex.

Olivier's Hamlet, very much a man of action, was admired for its pulsating vitality; for its sardonic humour and tenderness; for its naturalism and speed; for its intelligence and grace; for its magnetism and muscularity. There was, however, one major criticism:

He lacks music. He speaks the verse with facility; but hearing it in his mouth, I would just as soon it were prose.
W.A. Darlington *The Daily Telegraph*

Mr. Olivier does not speak poetry badly. He does not speak it at all.
James Agate *The Sunday Times*

49 *Fire Over England* 1937

Raymond Massey as Philip of Spain and Laurence Olivier as the English spy who uncovers the plans for the Armada, in *Fire Over England*, a film directed by William K. Howard.

Olivier's role was in the swashbuckling Errol Flynn manner and he insisted on doing his own stunts. The film was much admired by Adolf Hitler.

50 *Twelfth Night* 1937

Laurence Olivier as Sir Toby Belch and Ivy St Helier as Maria in Shakespeare's *Twelfth Night*, directed by Tyrone Guthrie at the Old Vic Theatre.

Olivier as Sir Toby Belch, in the first of his many brilliant disguises, and in the first of his many famous noses, blatantly played to the gallery in an outrageously amusing, cakes-and-ale, over-the-top performance, full of farcical acrobatic business; some critics saw an embryonic Falstaff, a role he was, sadly, never to act.

51 *Henry V 1937*

52 *Hamlet 1937*

Laurence Olivier as Henry and Jessica Tandy as Katharine in Shakespeare's *Henry V*, directed by Tyrone Guthrie at the Old Vic Theatre.

Shakespeare's *Henry V* was an odd choice for an actor and a director, who, in the climate of the late 1930s, were out of sympathy with the play's jingoism. In 1963 it was possible for John Barton and Trevor Nunn to direct the play as they might direct Bertolt Brecht's *Mother Courage*, and turn it into an anti-war tract, but in 1937, the year of George VI's Coronation, the Old Vic audiences would expect something a bit more patriotic. Olivier turned to the friend he always turned to for advice and Ralph Richardson said, 'I know he's a boring old schoolmaster on the face of it, but being Shakespeare he's the exaltation of all scoutmasters. He's the cold bath king, and you have to glory in it.'

Laurence Olivier as Hamlet and Vivien Leigh as Ophelia in Shakespeare's *Hamlet*, directed by Tyrone Guthrie at Kronborg Castle, Denmark.

At the invitation of the Danish Tourist Board, *Hamlet* went to Elsinore. Unfortunately for the company, the castle remained open to visitors all day and so they had to rehearse from midnight until six in the morning. On the opening night, there was such a downpour of rain that the production, instead of being staged in the castle courtyard, had to be improvised, in the round, in the Marienlyst Hotel's ballroom.

53 *Macbeth* 1937

Judith Anderson as Lady Macbeth and Laurence Olivier as Macbeth in Shakespeare's *Macbeth*, directed by Michel Saint-Denis at the Old Vic Theatre.

Watching his Macbeth, in an over-stylized interpretation, James Agate predicted that he would probably be twice as good when he was twice as old. Eighteen years later, at Stratford-upon-Avon, Olivier played Macbeth with resounding success.

You hear Macbeth's first line, then Larry's make-up comes on, then Banquo comes on, then Larry comes on.

Vivien Leigh

Mr. Olivier has fire and an admirable precision in declamation. His words have wings; nothing that he says or does lacks interest; and if it was not always in his power to dominate events, that was hardly his fault. This production seemed to me to be overweighted with

decoration, and lacking in true self-confidence. At crucial moments Macbeth had strange clothes to wear, and crowns under which any head might lie uneasy.

Harold Hobson *The Sunday Times*

Mr. Olivier gives us the poetry and the neurotic agony, but not the fierce strength which must accompany them. By far the best moment is after Duncan's murder, when he is all unstrung, his practical powers swamped in the surging crowd of images.

J.E. Sewell *The Daily Telegraph*

Macbeth is a notoriously unlucky play for actors. This production proved no exception. Not only did it have to be postponed at the very last minute from the Tuesday to the Friday, being technically not ready to open, but Lilian Baylis, founder of the Old Vic and Sadler's Wells, died on the Thursday.

54 *Twenty-One Days* 1937

Laurence Olivier and Esme Percy in *Twenty-One Days*, a film directed by Basil Dean.

Olivier played an eminent barrister's brother who accidentally kills the supposed husband of the girl he loves.

Adapted by Graham Greene from John Galsworthy's *The First and the Last, Twenty-One Days* was considered so awful that it was shelved for two years. When they finally saw it, Olivier and Vivien Leigh walked out of the cinema, and Graham Greene, who was film critic on the *Spectator*, hadn't a good word for it and apologized to his readers.

55 *The Divorce of Lady X* 1938

Laurence Olivier and Merle Oberon in *The Divorce of Lady X*, a film directed by Tim Whelan.

Olivier played a divorce lawyer who finds himself compromised in a hotel bedroom. The poster asked: '"Who was the *lady* in Room 315?" Mayfair boiled with gossip ... as the frantic young woman-hater combed the town to find the nameless beauty who had stolen his pajamas and his bed.' Merle Oberon and Olivier acted with wit and style.

56 *Othello 1938*

Laurence Olivier as Iago in Shakespeare's *Othello*, directed by Tyrone Guthrie at the Old Vic Theatre. Ralph Richardson played Othello.

Olivier and Guthrie, full of theories about the psychological relation of Iago and Othello, again sought advice from Dr Ernest Jones. He argued that Iago is subconsciously in love with Othello, an idea which immediately appealed to Olivier, but not, unfortunately, to Ralph Richardson who did not wish to be party to any homosexual interpretation of the play, and so the production never worked.

There was here none of the zest in evil for its own sake which Iago must disclose.
        W.A. Darlington *The Daily Telegraph*

He plays the part for comedy. This is a rattling Iago, an undergraduate at his pranks.
        The Times

Mr. Olivier might show his fangs more in his soliloquies, and he must really not throw good lines over his shoulder in his too conversational manner.
        Ivor Brown *The Observer*

57 *The King of Nowhere 1938*

Laurence Olivier in James Bridie's *The King of Nowhere*, directed by Tyrone Guthrie at the Old Vic Theatre.

Olivier played a mentally deranged actor who has escaped from an asylum and is persuaded by a rich and idealistic spinster to become the leader of a neo-Fascist party.

Mr. Laurence Olivier's is a revealing performance, sometimes too dancing, too spectacularly bright, but a shrewd portrait of this man whose tragedy is that, except in the parts he plays, he is without identity.
        The Times

58 *Coriolanus 1938*

Gordon Miller as young Marcius, Sybil Thorndike as Volumnia, Vivienne Bennett as Virgilia and Laurence Olivier as Coriolanus in Shakespeare's *Coriolanus*, directed by Lewis Casson at the Old Vic Theatre.

His Coriolanus was a study in arrested development: the victim of his own violent temper and the victim of a nature which seemingly forced him into situations in which he must actively antagonize the very people whose support he needed. Olivier played the role with sardonic humour, soaring insolence and, in the scenes with his mother, great tenderness. His spectacular death-fall had the audience on its feet, cheering wildly.

There is no doubt in my mind that the only sign of a great actor in the making in England today is Laurence Olivier. . . . If one has any reservation at all, it is to suggest that this steadily improving actor should abandon that make-up like a Javanese mask and trust more to his own features. At present his face is not so much made-up as buried beneath loam and plaster.

James Agate *The Sunday Times*

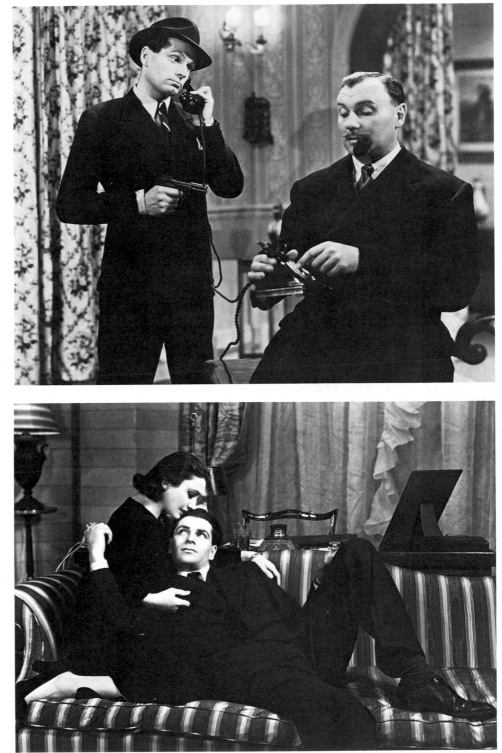

59 *Q Planes 1939*

Laurence Olivier as the spy and Ralph Richardson as the secret serviceman in *Q Planes*, a film directed by Tim Whelan. The US title is *Clouds Over Europe*.

60 *No Time For Comedy 1939*

Katharine Cornell and Laurence Olivier in S.N. Behrman's *No Time For Comedy*, directed by Guthrie McClintic at the Ethel Barrymore Theatre on Broadway, New York.

Olivier played a playwright who has to justify writing comedy in a world threatened by war.

61 *Wuthering Heights* *1939*

David Niven as Edgar, Donald Crisp as Dr Kenneth, Laurence Olivier as Heathcliff, Flora Robson as Ellen Dean and Merle Oberon as Cathy in the film version of Emily Brontë's *Wuthering Heights*, directed by William Wyler.

Olivier was a strikingly handsome, surprisingly well-spoken, gentle stable-boy; there was none of Heathcliff's passionate rage, only his inner heart-break. He was no brute at all. The performance was in keeping with the film's romantic approach which ignored the novel's savagery and Gothic grandeur. The sobbing anguish of 'Come in! Come in! Cathy, do come!' was beautifully done and the death-bed scene might have been out of *La Traviata*.

Laurence Olivier's Heathcliff is the man. He has Heathcliff's broad lowering brow, his scowl, his churlishness, the wild tenderness, the bearing, speech, and manner of the demon-possessed.

New York Times

How much better they would have made Wuthering Heights *in France. They know there how to shoot sexual passion; but in this Californian-constructed Yorkshire, among the sensitive neurotic English voices, sex is cellophaned; there is no egotism, no obsession. This Heathcliff would never have married for revenge (Mr. Olivier's nervous, breaking voice belongs to balconies and Verona and romantic love), and one cannot imagine the ghost of this Cathy weeping with balked passion outside the broken window.*

Graham Greene *Spectator*

62 *Rebecca* 1940

C. Aubrey Smith, Laurence Olivier, Joan Fontaine, George Sanders and Judith Anderson in the film version of Daphne du Maurier's *Rebecca*, directed by Alfred Hitchcock.

Larry's silent action and reactions become slower as his dialogue becomes faster, each day. His pauses and spacing on the scene with the girl in which she tells him about the ball are the most ungodly slow and deliberate reactions I have ever seen. It is played as though he were deciding whether or not to run for President instead of whether or not to give a ball. And for God's sake, speed up Larry not merely in these close-ups, but in the rest of the picture on his reactions, which are apparently the way he plays on the stage, where it could be satisfactory. But while you are at it, you will have to keep your ears open to make sure that we know what the hell he's talking about, because he still has a tendency to speed up his words and to read them in such a way that an American audience can't understand them.

David O. Selznick in a memo to Alfred Hitchcock

Laurence Olivier is admirably suited to the role of Maxim de Winter, playing it with a moody intensity that is exactly right.

Cinema

Laurence Olivier is excellent as the sardonic Maxim and makes him credible and not unsympathetic.

Monthly Film Bulletin

63 *Romeo and Juliet* 1940

Vivien Leigh as Juliet and Laurence Olivier as Romeo in Shakespeare's *Romeo and Juliet*, directed by Laurence Olivier at the 51st Street Theatre, New York.

The superficiality of his acting is difficult to understand. He is mannered and affected, avoiding directness in even simple episodes. In costumes that flare extravagantly at the shoulders, he looks like a belligerent sparrow when he scurries across the stage. Most of the time he speaks for Juliet's private ear, *dropping his voice at the end of lines as though they did not matter. As his own director Mr. Olivier has never heard himself in the performance. That is just as well; he would be astonished if he did. . . .*
Brooks Atkinson *New York Times*

The reviews were so bad that there were queues of people round the block asking for their money back. The Oliviers lost all their savings.

64 *Pride and Prejudice 1940*

Greer Garson as Elizabeth Bennett, Edward Ashley as Mr Wickham, Laurence Olivier as Mr Darcy and E.E. Clive as Sir William Lucas in the film version of Jane Austen's *Pride and Prejudice*, directed by Robert Z. Leonard.

In 1935 in his curtain speech on the first night of *Golden Arrow*, Olivier had predicted Greer Garson would be a star. Some theatre critics, feeling that he was doing their job for them, were irritated by his remarks. Four years later he and Greer Garson were working together again in Hollywood and *both* were international stars.

Pride and Prejudice was Olivier's third film success in a row: wearing the Regency costume with becoming ease and grace, his proud Darcy cut a dashing figure.

65 *Lady Hamilton 1941*

Vivien Leigh as Emma and Laurence Olivier as Lord Nelson in *Lady Hamilton*, a film directed by Alexander Korda. The US title is *That Hamilton Woman*.

It was Winston Churchill who suggested to Alexander Korda that he make a film about Lord Nelson; and he may well have had a hand in the script. Certainly the parallels with the situation in 1941 were underlined. The American censors objected to *That Hamilton Woman*, which they saw as propaganda for both war and adultery. The Red Army, apparently more broadminded, adopted Vivien Leigh as their pin-up girl.

66 *49th Parallel 1941*

Raymond Lovell, Laurence Olivier, Finlay Currie and Eric Portman in *49th Parallel*, a propaganda film commissioned by the Ministry of Information and directed by Michael Powell. The US title is *The Invaders*.

Olivier played a French-Canadian trapper in an Eskimo village; he is shot by members of a German U-boat crew, stranded in Canada and trying to escape to America.

67 *The Demi-Paradise 1943*

Wilfred Hyde White, Laurence Olivier and Penelope Dudley Ward in *The Demi-Paradise*, a propaganda film directed by Anthony Asquith. The US title is *Adventure for Two*.

Olivier played a Russian engineer who visits England before and then during the war.

68 *Peer Gynt 1944*

Ralph Richardson as Peer and Laurence Olivier as the Button-Moulder in Henrik Ibsen's *Peer Gynt*, directed by Tyrone Guthrie and Robert Helpmann at the New Theatre.

Towards the end of the war, Lord Lytton, Chairman of the Old Vic governors, wrote to the First Lord of the Admiralty requesting the release of Ralph Richardson and Laurence Olivier from the Fleet Air Arm so that the Old Vic might re-open at the New Theatre, their own theatre having been bombed in 1940. They were joined by John Burrell and the 1944/1945/1946 seasons passed into theatrical legend, establishing Olivier – snatching the crown held until then by John Gielgud – as the greatest English actor of his times.

The first season opened with Ibsen's *Peer Gynt*. Olivier made a brief and chilling appearance, right at the end of the play, in the small but unforgettable role of the Button-Moulder who comes to melt Peer down.

69 *Arms and the Man* 1944

Ralph Richardson as Captain Bluntschli, Laurence Olivier as Major Sergius Saranoff and Margaret Leighton as Raina in Bernard Shaw's *Arms and the Man*, directed by John Burrell at the New Theatre.

Sergius is a humbug, buffoon, blackguard and coward. He is an amateur soldier – more like an operatic tenor, really – who so absurdly, yet so successfully, charges artillery on horseback and becomes the hero of the hour. Though he is always striking heroic and romantic attitudes, he actually does know the truth about war:

'The dream of patriots and heroes! A fraud – a hollow sham like love.'

Spurred and moustached, Olivier was abominably and swaggeringly conceited; initially he had difficulty in playing him ('a bloody awful part') until Tyrone Guthrie suggested that he would never succeed in the role unless he learned to love Sergius. Olivier has claimed that this was the richest piece of advice he ever had and that it changed his whole approach to acting.

70 *Richard III* 1944

Ralph Richardson as Richmond and Laurence Olivier as Richard in Shakespeare's *Richard III*, directed by John Burrell at the New Theatre.

If there was one role more than any other which established Olivier's greatness, then that role was his Richard III; it was a huge success with the public, the critics and the profession itself. John Gielgud, after seeing his performance, presented him with the very sword Edmund Kean had used in the part. Olivier played a virtuoso villain with electrifying theatricality: he was witty in his ironic observation of the action, terrifying in his screaming rage, nerve-racking in his brooding silences, pathetic in his cry, 'Nobody loves me', and chilling in his animal-like writhing on the ground in death. The performance has passed into twentieth-century theatrical consciousness and fortunately it is preserved on film.

As he made his way downstage very slowly and with odd interruptions in his progress, he seemed malignity incarnate. All the complication of Richard's character – its cruelty, its ambition, its sardonic humour seemed implicit in his expression and his walk, so that when at last he reached the front of the stage and began his speech, all that he had to say of his evil purpose seemed to us in the audience less like a revelation than a confirmation of something we had already been told.

W.A. Darlington *The Daily Telegraph*

A Saturday matinée of Richard III *at the Tivoli Theatre, Sydney, in 1948 was my first encounter with Laurence Olivier on stage. The auditorium was not air-conditioned, and as the lights dimmed the audience made it clear that they were serious about coughing. You can't, however, cough and laugh at the same time. So their first set-back was the discovery not only that* Richard III *is a frequently funny play but that it was in the hands of a superlative comedian. Later on, when Richard pulls rank on an astonished Buckingham and forces him to his knees, they stopped coughing for another reason; there was a chill in the house better than any air-conditioning.*

After the interval, as the noose of the play tightened around its protagonist, we became aware that we were in the presence of something as serious as a sporting event and twice as absorbing; a contest in which the ball was never dropped nor a kick missed. On came Richard, a bottled spider, and the entire theatre seemed to hum like a pitchfork as he exclaimed, 'A Horse! A Horse! My Kingdom for a horse!' The hackneyed line, butt of a thousand schoolboy jokes, suddenly meant a dozen things at once. You knew from that despairing cry (a collision of longing and practicality which has so often been the hallmark of the great Olivier moments) that the horse was the Sherman tank of its day and that the outcome of the battle depended on it. You knew that Richard quite literally meant what he said; that he would trade his life's achievement for a mount. You knew, also, that a horse would not be forthcoming and that the game was over. It was only a matter of time before Richard would meet his end in a series of ghastly spasms like a poisoned dog.

It was these shafts of intuitive understanding into the raw life beneath the text, realized with indelible theatrical daring, that in my lifetime have made an Olivier performance the most irresistible reason for shutting your front door and setting off for the theatre. It was something you would never find on the printed page at home. You had to be there, spellbound with the others.

Michael Blakemore

71 *Uncle Vanya 1945*

Margaret Leighton as Yelena and Laurence Olivier as Astrov in Anton Chekhov's *Uncle Vanya*, directed by John Burrell at the New Theatre.

Mr. Laurence Olivier's Astrov becomes, as it advances, a very distinguished portrait, in which superficial weakness and underlying strength are brought out in their proper proportions.
The Times

A magnificently witty and feeling performance.
James Agate *The Sunday Times*

It is a great relief to have the doctor played straight and not turned into a vodka-swilling character-part, all shaggy, maudlin, super-Chekhovian charm.
Ivor Brown *The Observer*

Astrov was one of Olivier's favourite roles and he returned to it again, seventeen years later, in the opening season of the Chichester Festival Theatre.

72 *Henry V 1945*

Laurence Olivier as Henry, Renee Asherson as Katharine and Ivy St Helier as Alice in the film version of Shakespeare's *Henry V*, directed by Laurence Olivier.

73 *Henry V 1945*

Laurence Olivier as Henry V in his film of Shakespeare's play.

The film was a worldwide success with the critics and the public and won Olivier an Oscar for his outstanding achievement as actor, director and producer. The success was due in part to the timing of the film: the Saint Crispin day speech, tempered by the anxiety on the eve of battle, perfectly caught and matched the nation's wartime mood.

Olivier, by setting the opening English court scenes within the rough confines of the wooden O of Shakespeare's Globe and then by acting the French court scenes within the delicate artificiality of designs, clearly influenced by *Les Très Riches Heures du Duc de Berry*, always emphasizes that we are watching a play. But when it comes to the Battle of Agincourt, played out on the vasty fields of Ireland to William Walton's music – which in its rhythm and editing is comparable to Eisenstein's and Prokofiev's *Alexander Nevsky* – his *Henry V* is pure cinema.

The movies have produced one of their rare great works of art. Almost continually, it invests the art of Shakespeare – and the art of cinema as well – with a new spaciousness, a new mobility, a new radiance. Sometimes by courageous (but never revolutionary) cuts, rearrangements and interpolations, it improves on the original. Yet its brilliance is graceful, never self-assertive. It simply subserves, extends, illuminates, and liberates Shakespeare's poem. One of the prime joys of the picture is the spring-water freshness and immediacy of the lines, the lack of antiquarian culture-clogging. Especially as spoken by Olivier, the lines constantly combine the power of prose and the glory of poetry.

Time Magazine

His Henry stood out with the bright, bold colors of the English standard. In speech, appearance, posture, thought, and feeling, his Henry was a performance of superlative merit. He shone with spiritual splendor, a quality as rare in actors as it is in other human beings.

John Mason Brown *Saturday Review of Literature*

74 *Henry IV Part I 1945*

Ralph Richardson as Falstaff and Laurence Olivier as Hotspur in Shakespeare's *Henry IV Part I*, directed by John Burrell at the New Theatre.

The two parts of *Henry IV* offered the first of Olivier's dazzling transformations that season: the ginger-wigged, virile, hot-tempered, impatient, passionate, stammering Hotspur was followed by a feeble and quavering scarecrow of an old man, the bearded hermit, Shallow, a starved Justice of the Peace.

The stutter – and the stutter on the letter 'w' in particular – was rooted in the Shakespearian text and it made Hotspur's last lines

> *No, Percy, thou art dust,*
> *And food for –*

even more poignant as Olivier struggled to say 'worms' and died, failing to do so.

75 *Henry IV Part II 1945*

Brian Parker as the Page, Michael Raghan as Bardolph, Laurence Olivier as Justice Shallow and Miles Malleson as Silence in Shakespeare's *Henry IV Part II*, directed by John Burrell at the New Theatre.

76 *Oedipus Rex* 1945

Laurence Olivier as Oedipus and Sybil Thorndike as Jocasta in Sophocles' *Oedipus Rex*, directed by Michel Saint-Denis at the New Theatre.

Olivier's famous 'Oh! Oh!' when the full catalogue of his sins is unfolded must still be resounding in some high recess of the New Theatre's dome: some stick of wood must still, I feel, be throbbing from it. The two cries were torn from beyond tears or shame or guilt: they came from the stomach, with all the ecstatic grief and fright of a newborn baby's wail. The point is not whether these crazy sobs were 'tricks' or whether or not they were necessary to the part: the point is that they were overwhelming experiences, and that no other actor in England could have carried them off. A man seeing the horrors of infinity in a trance might make such a sound: a man awaking from a nightmare to find a truth might make such a sound; but no other man, and no other actor.

Kenneth Tynan *He That Plays The King*

77 *Oedipus Rex 1945*

Laurence Olivier in Sophocles' *Oedipus Rex*, directed by Michel Saint-Denis at the New Theatre.

Laurence Olivier grows in stature before our eyes. His intelligence sheds radiance upon everything he touches. Here is an actor who refuses to repeat himself but brings to each role a freshness and an understanding that leaves us wondering if anything is beyond his reach.

Beverley Baxter *Evening Standard*

One of those performances in which blood and electricity are somehow mixed. It pulls down lightning from the sky. It is as awesome, dwarfing and appalling as one of nature's angriest displays.

John Mason Brown *Saturday Review of Literature*

78 *The Critic 1945*

John Garley as the Prompter, George Relph as Mr Dangle and Laurence Olivier as Mr Puff in Richard Brinsley Sheridan's *The Critic*, a burlesque of eighteenth-century heroic tragedy, directed by Miles Malleson at the New Theatre.

Olivier's outrageous Puff, the gossip columnist turned author, tossed snuff into the air and bashed his head against the walls of the stage box when his play was cut and threatened to print every word. Finally, he was caught up on a piece of scenery and disappeared up into the flies, to the consternation of all, only to return on a cloud.

Olivier, acting Oedipus and Puff on the same evening, going from one extreme to another, is such a famous bit of theatrical legend, that it comes as a surprise to find that so many critics objected to the double bill. James Agate even went so far as to claim that the performance of *The Critic* had driven everything about *Oedipus Rex* from his mind.

79 *King Lear 1946*

Alec Guinness as the Fool and Laurence Olivier as Lear in Shakespeare's *King Lear*, directed by Laurence Olivier at the New Theatre.

The production was notable for the unexpected humour of the abdication scene and the old man's total lack of senility. It was always hoped that Olivier would return to the role when he was older but unfortunately he did not come back to it until he was well into his seventies.

There was once a time when Mr. Olivier was all violence, all extreme passion; like Kean, he was constantly upon the rack. But, as his passion has strengthened and his expression of it ripened, so has it grown more controlled. There are moments in his performance of Lear that are of utter stillness and of quiet pathos. The same power that can set the storm in motion can now calm it by the lifting of a hand.

Harold Hobson *The Sunday Times*

Olivier is a player of unparalleled animal powers miraculously crossed with a player of extreme technical cuteness. . . . Instead of the pathos of crumbling strength, he offered the misfortune of bright wits blurred. He could not give us more than a fraction of all the massive, deluded grandeur.

Kenneth Tynan *He That Plays The King*

80 *King Lear 1946*

Joyce Redman as Cordelia, Harry Andrews as Cornwall, Margaret Leighton as Regan, Laurence Olivier as Lear, Nicholas Hannen as Kent, Pamela Brown as Goneril and Cecil Winter as Albany in Shakespeare's *King Lear*.

I shall never forget Larry's generosity in helping me to get back in the theatre after the war. I had first acted with him in John Gielgud's production of Romeo and Juliet *in 1935. To this day, he still reminds me of our duel. He was playing Mercutio, I was playing Tybalt, and we really did have such a bash that we injured each other every night!*

In 1945, he cast me as Cornwall in King Lear *and he (having been to an eye specialist) demonstrated exactly how he wanted me to pluck out Gloucester's eyes. It was pretty horrendous. He then invited Margaret Leighton, who was playing Regan, to have an orgasm while I was trampling on the eyes. After the first night, with the audience fainting and being taken away, he agreed we had gone over the top and toned it down a bit. Larry, a very physical person, always has relished the physical aspects of acting.*

Harry Andrews

81 *Hamlet* 1948

Laurence Olivier as Hamlet in his film of Shakespeare's play.

82 *Hamlet* 1948

Jean Simmons as Ophelia and Laurence Olivier as Hamlet in the film version of Shakespeare's *Hamlet*.

    Hamlet, described by Olivier as an essay in Hamlet ('the tragedy of a man who could not make up his mind') and the most criticized of his three Shakespearian films, now seems by far the best *film*. Stunningly photographed in black and white by Desmond Dickinson, it looks like a great silent masterpiece with a beautifully spoken,

dubbed soundtrack. The action in Roger Furse's huge set is always *theatrical* Shakespeare and, as a record of how Shakespeare used to be acted, invaluable. The opening soliloquy is particularly effective in the cinema when the inner voice, thinking his father 'but two months dead' is immediately corrected by a sharp and aloud, 'nay not so much, not two'.

To some it will be one of the greatest films ever made, to others a deep disappointment. Laurence Olivier leaves no doubt that he is one of our greatest living actors. His rich, moving voice, his expressive face, make of the tortured Dane a figure of deep and sincere tragedy. Arguments about his age and his blond hair cannot detract from the personal triumph of his performance. His liberties with the text, however, are sure to disturb many.

Milton Shulman *Evening Standard*

83 *The Skin of Our Teeth 1948*

Vivien Leigh as Sabina and Eileen Beldon, Terence Morgan, Georgina Jumel and Laurence Olivier as the Antrobus family in Thornton Wilder's history of the world, *The Skin of Our Teeth*, directed by Laurence Olivier.

In 1945, Vivien Leigh had scored a huge personal success in this allegory, which is a mixture of highbrow tomfoolery, anachronisms and stage mishaps.

Olivier revived the production in 1948, when he and Vivien Leigh led the Old Vic Company on a ten-month tour of Australia and New Zealand in a repertoire which also included *Richard III* and *The School for Scandal*.

84 *The School for Scandal 1948*

Vivien Leigh and Laurence Olivier as Lady and Sir Peter Teazle in Richard Brinsley Sheridan's *The School for Scandal*, directed by Laurence Olivier on the Old Vic tour of Australia and New Zealand, followed by a season in London at the New Theatre in 1949.

Sheridan's play is a mixture of mischief and sentiment in which, surprisingly, the sentiment wears better; the scandalmongers merely bitch about people we do not know.

Olivier's Sir Peter started from the premise that he really did love his wife ('How happy I should be if I could tease her into loving me') and he went unashamedly for the pathos. It was a touching, endearing, loveable performance, genial and wistful.

In that disillusioned, sore-tried ex-bachelor, he has found not a figure of fun, but a creature of infinite (and inhibited) melancholy; not a verbal sparring partner for his spirited young wife, but a gentle spoken, sweetly smiling philosopher. A performance of masterly sensitiveness by Olivier.

Harold Conway *Evening Standard*

The acting is stylized to such a pitch that I felt on occasion as though I were at a ballet rather than a serious comedy and as a result Sir Laurence achieved decorative effect at the expense of dramatic power.

W.A. Darlington *The Daily Telegraph*

85 *Antigone 1949*

Hugh Stewart and Thomas Heathcote as the guards, Vivien Leigh as
Antigone, George Relph as Creon, Michael Reddington as a page,
Laurence Olivier as Chorus, Helen Beck as Eurydice and Eileen
Beldon as Nurse in Jean Anouilh's *Antigone*, directed by Laurence
Olivier at the New Theatre.

When Anouilh's play was first produced in France during the war,
the French were quick to identify with the heroine, seeing her stand
against Creon as a symbol of their own struggle against the German
occupation. Olivier, immaculate in white tie and tails, commenting
on the action and offering a fine definition of modern tragedy, gave a
performance that was both dry and menacing.

86 *Venus Observed 1950*

Denholm Elliott as Edgar, George Relph as Reedbeck, Heather Stannard as Perpetua, Laurence Olivier as the Duke of Altair and Brenda de Banzie as Jessie in Christopher Fry's *Venus Observed*, directed by Laurence Olivier at the St James's Theatre.

In 1949 Olivier became an actor-manager and acquired the lease of the St James's Theatre. He commissioned Christopher Fry, who was having a huge success with *The Lady's Not For Burning*, to write a play for him. *Venus Observed*, the second of the author's seasonal comedies, is an autumnal piece. Olivier, urbane, soldierly and brittle, played the Duke of Altair, who, after a lifetime of philandering, decides he must marry one of three women and asks his son to take on the role of Paris.

I gave Laurence Olivier an anxious time before I finished Venus Observed, *which was to open his management at the St James's Theatre in 1950. The date for rehearsals to begin was getting uncomfortably close, and he had read only the first act. I wrote to tell him that I had got to the end of the second act, and would type it out and send it to him by the end of the week. But by then I was into Act 3 and unwilling to break off while I typed Act 2. After a patient silence, a parcel came from Olivier containing a typewriter ribbon (far too big for my 1917 portable Corona), a brush to clean the keys and an eraser, with a message which I have beside me as I write: 'Let me know if there is anything else you need, won't you? I'm not making you nervous, am I? I do hope I'm not making you nervous.'*

Christopher Fry

87 *Caesar and Cleopatra* 1951

Niall MacGinnis as Rufio, Laurence Olivier as Caesar, Robert Helpmann as Apollodorus, Cy Grant as the Nubian Sentinel and Vivien Leigh as Cleopatra in Bernard Shaw's *Caesar and Cleopatra*, directed by Michael Benthall at the St James's Theatre. It played in tandem with *Antony and Cleopatra* and both productions transferred to the Ziegfield Theatre in New York at the end of 1951.

Sir Laurence, subduing the natural fire and animal force of his personality, presents a soldier still active, but weary of war, ready at any moment to fight victoriously but without any zest, the élan and abandonment of youth gone, and only the grey, cold, frightening strength remaining.

Harold Hobson *The Sunday Times*

It is a personal triumph for Sir Laurence, who is excellently dry and persuasive as the Caesar of clement philosophy and yet resonant as roused soldier; he wears his lean years like a grey mantle.

Manchester Guardian

Here was the perfect picture – the man conscious of the loneliness of greatness, the futility of passion, the uselessness of vengeance for insult or retaliation for treachery.

W.A. Darlington *The Daily Telegraph*

His is a steely stage personality and it gives a terrifying edge to all Caesar's intellectual magnanimities and gentle philosophizing.

The Times

88 *Antony and Cleopatra 1951*

Laurence Olivier and Vivien Leigh in Shakespeare's *Antony and Cleopatra*, directed by Michael Benthall at the St James's Theatre.

Sir Laurence's Antony, gracefully bearded, passionately vacillating, passes with accomplishment from doting amorousness, through gusts of nervous optimism, to fierce despair. This performance is more showy and less impressive than his Caesar.
Harold Hobson *The Sunday Times*

Sir Laurence is a lightweight, charming and somewhat too dry Antony who certainly does not overload the lover's sighs.
Philip Hope-Wallace *Manchester Guardian*

In the last two acts of Antony and Cleopatra *Shakespeare wrote as never before or after. To see them performed with a majesty equal to their mighty utterance of desire, ecstasy, despair and the brave end has been my life's desire in the theatre, and now I have seen it done.*
Ivor Brown *The Observer*

89 *The Magic Box 1951*

Laurence Olivier and Jack Hulbert in *The Magic Box*, a film in celebration of William Friese-Greene, the inventor of moving pictures, directed by John Boulting.

The film set a precedent for stars appearing in cameo roles in British films; Olivier, as the Holborn policeman, who is dragged in by the excited inventor (Robert Donat) to see the magic box working for the first time, shares the best and most moving scene in Eric Ambler's screenplay.

90 *Carrie 1952*

Laurence Olivier in the film version of Theodore Dreiser's *Carrie*, directed by William Wyler.

Olivier played the restaurant manager, so obsessed with the woman he loves that he ends up in the flop-house, degraded and broken.

When word first came through that Mr. Olivier had been cast in the difficult role of this reckless Chicago gentleman out of America's raw Gilded Age, there were those who regarded this selection as a perilously chancy choice, likely to lead to a distortion that would throw the whole story askew. The eminent British actor was thought too elegant and alien for the role of Mr. Dreiser's middle-aged hero who went to ruin out of love for a pretty girl. Mr. Olivier gives the film its closest contact with the book.

New York Times

91 *The Beggar's Opera* 1953

Dorothy Tutin as Polly Peachum and Laurence Olivier as Captain Macheath in a film version of John Gay's ballad opera, *The Beggar's Opera*, a Newgate pastoral directed by Peter Brook.

Olivier's highwayman and gamester was an amiable, charming, sexy villain, who rode in triumph to Tyburn; but his singing voice was not really up to it and since he and Stanley Holloway (playing Peachum) were the only actors who were not dubbed by professional singers, he felt the shortcomings of his light baritone voice were emphasized all the more.

92 *The Sleeping Prince 1953*

Richard Wattis as the English attaché, Vivien Leigh as Mary Morgan, an American chorus girl, Laurence Olivier as the Grand Duke Charles, Prince Regent of Carpathia and Paul Hardwick as the Major-Domo in Terence Rattigan's *The Sleeping Prince*, an occasional fairy tale for Coronation year, directed by Laurence Olivier at the Phoenix Theatre.

The comedy is the stuff of which Ruritanian musicals are made, only without the music. Olivier, as the gruff and monocled Balkan Prince Uncharming who attempts to seduce an American chorus girl, was generally thought to be wasting his time.

93 *Twelfth Night 1955*

Laurence Olivier as Malvolio in Shakespeare's *Twelfth Night*, directed by John Gielgud at the Memorial Theatre, Stratford-upon-Avon.

Olivier's Malvolio became the leading role: nasal and lisping, he stewarded with fussing efficiency, making the cross-gartered puritanical ass into an effeminate, somewhat vulgar social climber, with permed hair and affected speech, uncertain how to pronounce 'slough' as in 'cast thy humble slough and appear fresh'. At the end of the play, the whirligig of time having brought its revenges, he cut the laughter to make the comedy his personal tragedy.

94 *Macbeth 1955*

Laurence Olivier as Macbeth and Vivien Leigh as Lady Macbeth in Shakespeare's *Macbeth*, directed by Glen Byam Shaw at the Memorial Theatre, Stratford-upon-Avon.

95 *Macbeth 1955*

Keith Michell (standing left) as Macduff, Laurence Olivier as Macbeth and Vivien Leigh as Lady Macbeth in Shakespeare's *Macbeth*.

Olivier's performance re-established his pre-eminence in the profession. He opened in a quiet key, at pains to be worthy of Duncan's high opinion; trapped by his ambition into a murder to which he was not fully committed, he was appalled by what he had done. Once king, however, he played the tyrant with ruthless authority and, in his scene with the two murderers, an almost Richard III-like humour. Olivier always made Macbeth fully aware of his tragedy and most movingly so on the lines:

> *I am in blood*
> *Stepp'd so far that should I wade no more*
> *Returning were as tedious as go o'er.*

Later in the play he was to take the line to the doctor, 'Canst thou not minister to a mind diseased?' and turn it into a question about himself rather than Lady Macbeth.

96 *Titus Andronicus 1955*

Laurence Olivier as Titus, Vivien Leigh as Lavinia and Alan Webb as Marcus in Shakespeare's *Titus Andronicus*, directed by Peter Brook at the Memorial Theatre, Stratford-upon-Avon. In 1957 the production toured Europe, followed by a season at the Stoll Theatre in London.

The rarely performed *Titus Andronicus* was a supper of horrors, an unnerving night of the long knives. Peter Brook, by cutting and rearranging the text, sought to persuade the audience that what they were watching was not Grand Guignol but High Roman Tragedy; the audience fainted at every performance and extra St John's ambulance volunteers had to be called in.

Even though Titus is just as lacking in humanity as everybody else in this slaughterhouse, Olivier, in his rashness, rage and craziness, underlined the Lear-like parallels and forced us to pity Titus, never more so than when he was confronted by his daughter, the mutilated and raped Lavinia:

> *What fool hath added water to the sea?*
> *Or brought a faggot to bright-burning Troy?*
> *My grief was at the height before thou cam'st.*

There was another memorable moment when Marcus asked him why he should laugh at his griefs and, in a flash of sanity in his madness, he replied: 'Why I have not another tear to shed.'

97 *Titus Andronicus 1955*

Laurence Olivier as Titus and Vivien Leigh as Lavinia in Shakespeare's *Titus Andronicus*.

Sir Laurence's Titus, even with one hand gone, is a five finger exercise transformed into an unforgettable concerto of grief. This is a performance which ushers us into the presence of one who is, pound for pound, the greatest actor alive. As usual, he raises one's hair with the risks he takes. Titus enters not as a beaming hero but as a battered veteran, stubborn and shambling, long past caring about the people's cheers. A hundred campaigns have tanned his heart to leather, and from the cracking of that heart, there issues a terrible music, not untinged by madness. One hears great cries, which, like all of this actor's best effects, seem to have been dredged up from an ocean-bed of fatigue.

Kenneth Tynan *The Observer*

The two occasions when I worked with Larry touched two extremes. One experience was miserable, the other radiant. In one case – The Beggar's Opera *– we never agreed at any moment on anything – the result was a battlefield – and the work that emerged was bad for both of us. The second time –* Titus Andronicus *– we came together reluctantly and to our astonishment found ourselves in immediate harmony. So we did good work together. From these experiences, I learned that part of Larry's extraordinary force is that once he begins to move in a certain direction nothing in the world can change his course. I think that almost immediately when he reads a play he senses which way he wants to go and off he sets, slowly, suspiciously and remorselessly, removing all obstacles between himself and his goal. So is he directable? Yes and no. What matters clearly – and this depends more on luck than on discussion – he and the director must be on the same rails from the outset. In this case, there is no suspicion, no resistance. But if the intuitive sense of ultimate shape in the director's mind is different from that of the actor's, then no bridges can be made. Together we broke one bridge, but built another. It was worth it.*

Peter Brook

98 *Richard III 1955*

Laurence Olivier as Richard III in his film of Shakespeare's play.

Richard, a born actor, who revels in his role of Machiavellian villain, is always conscious of his theatrical effect on others. Olivier was never less than theatrical. His timing, as when he arrived late and inappropriately cheerful at Edward's death-bed, or when, having secured the crown, he forced his accomplices to kneel and kiss an extended gloved hand, was perfect.

The soliloquies were particularly successful. The opening, which drew on some of Richard's best lines in *Henry VI*, wittily established his character. Olivier, with a complacent smirk, a smack of the lips and a bat of the eyelids, immediately took the audience into his confidence. Off to court the Lady Anne, over her husband's coffin, he told us, with splendid piping irony, 'To her, go I, a jolly thriving wooer'; much later, having suffered a terrible nightmare on the eve of Bosworth, he leant towards the camera, as he mounted his horse to go into battle, and reassured us: 'Richard is himself again.'

There was a memorable exchange between him and Buckingham on Coronation Day when Buckingham, pushing his luck, came to claim his reward and was told, in no uncertain hysterical terms, 'I am not in the giving vein today'. The film is an excellent record of one of the definitive performances of our time.

99 *Richard III 1955*

Claire Bloom as Lady Anne and Laurence Olivier as Gloucester in the film version of Shakespeare's *Richard III*, directed by Laurence Olivier.

100 *Richard III 1955*

Laurence Olivier as Gloucester, newly crowned Richard III, and Ralph Richardson as Buckingham in the film version of Shakespeare's *Richard III*.

Laurence Olivier, supremely at his best when in complete control. My memory of him when he was acting and directing the film of Richard III *showed him as absolute master both of the stage and screen. His authority and expertise, as well as his sympathetic understanding of actors and crew, were a delight to see. An inspired comedian as Shallow and Mr Puff. He triumphed in two of the performances I most admired: Edgar in* The Dance of Death *and the broken-down actor in* The Entertainer; *and he was equally superb as Titus Andronicus. His Othello, Lear and Shylock (to say nothing of his Oedipus) were all moving and sometimes controversial. His versatility, dynamic energy and physical prowess, all these qualities, as well as his skill in directing and organization, make up an astonishing record in his wonderful career.*

John Gielgud

101 *The Entertainer 1957*

George Relph, Laurence Olivier and Joan Plowright in John
Osborne's *The Entertainer*, directed by Tony Richardson at the
Palace Theatre. The production, which had transferred from the
Royal Court Theatre, was seen at the Theatre Royale, New York, in
1958.

Olivier invited John Osborne to write a play for him. The result
was *The Entertainer*, in which the decline of England is mirrored in
the decline of the English music hall. 'Don't clap too hard, lady, it's
an old building.'

Archie Rice, a fifth-rate comedian ('I have a go, don't I?') is now
reduced to appearing in a twice-nightly nude show, filling in the
time before the girls come on. He camps about on stage to get a titter
out of his mutton-like audience in the same way that he camps about
at home to hide his true feelings.

'The one and only' Archie Rice, in his check suit, bowler, bow tie,
white socks, tap dancing and singing such songs as 'We're All Out
For Good Old Number One' and 'Thank God We're Normal', offers a
tired routine of queer jokes, cheap double-entendres and phoney
bonhomie. His private life, lecherous and boozing, is no less cynical
and hollow.

Olivier, however, by making Archie aware of his degradation, gave
him tragic stature. It was one of his greatest triumphs and a major
turning point in his career.

*The Entertainer is a remarkable role; and remarkably Larry played
it. But to do it eight performances a week? It seemed to me that he did
it with his feet. He trod the stage in a rhythm from beginning to end –
like a lonely jazz player – and each shift of weight, shuffle, had a
beat. His feet beat a rhythm to his brain which re-arranged,
transformed; and thus was dictated a marvellous and continuous
pattern, producing the power, the subtlety and the despair – all
through the beat of his feet.*

Dorothy Tutin

102 *The Prince and the Showgirl 1957*

Laurence Olivier and Marilyn Monroe in *The Prince and the
Showgirl*, the film version of Terence Rattigan's *The Sleeping Prince*,
directed by Laurence Olivier.

103 *John Gabriel Borkman 1958*

Laurence Olivier as Borkman and Anne Castaldini as Frida Foldal in
Henrik Ibsen's *John Gabriel Borkman*, directed for television by
Christopher Morahan.

Ibsen's penultimate play, a psychological and symbolic melodrama, which has an ice-cold, guilt-ridden brilliance, is essentially a
struggle for power, financial and emotional: a chilling confrontation
of obdurates, as hard as iron ore itself. Borkman is willing to sacrifice
everybody to his ambition – the woman he loved, his family, and finally
himself. He holds himself in perpetual readiness for the day when
society will go down on its bended knee and beg him to take up the
chairmanship of the bank once more. 'There is no precedent,' says a
friend, tactfully. 'Precedence is for ordinary people,' is the financier's
reply. Olivier was at his best in this scene with George Relph, who gave
a beautiful performance as Foldal.

104 *Coriolanus 1959*

Malcolm Ranson as young Marcius, Mary Ure as Virgilia, Edith Evans as Volumnia, Laurence Olivier as Coriolanus and Anthony Nicholls as Aufidius in Shakespeare's *Coriolanus*, directed by Peter Hall at the Memorial Theatre, Stratford-upon-Avon.

He presents a man whose pride and wilful judgement slowly obscure from him the truth that his narrow conception of honour has brought him to think of his country's good only as a ladder of his own reputation. It is the tragedy of an egoist.

The Times

Here, cursing the plebeians, he gave the phrases such a charge of emotion that he gathered them into a single rhetorical missile, so that the speech had an impact like jagged stones parcelled together and hurled in somebody's face. There was a bizarre impression of one man lynching a crowd.

Laurence Kitchin *Mid-Century Drama*

It is a performance which keeps the audience in thrall, lit with surprise and danger, unpredictable and alluring, and the death is overwhelmingly tragic.

Philip Hope-Wallace *Manchester Guardian*

105 *Coriolanus 1959*

The death of Coriolanus. Twenty years previously at the Old Vic, Olivier had hurled himself down a staircase, somersaulting and rolling over three times to arrive just short of the footlights. Now at the age of fifty-two, no less spectacularly, he fell off a high platform to be caught by the ankles by two soldiers, who left him hanging upside down, Mussolini-fashion.

106 *The Devil's Disciple 1959*

Laurence Olivier as General Burgoyne and Harry Andrews as Major
Swindon in the film version of Bernard Shaw's *The Devil's Disciple*,
directed by Guy Hamilton.

The best thing about the film is that it fulfils the wish of most
theatregoers who see Bernard Shaw's play: namely it gives them
more of General Burgoyne. It does this by the simple expedient of
spreading his part throughout the film instead of restricting it to the
court martial.

Shaw introduces Gentleman Johnny to his readers thus: 'His eyes,
large, brilliant, apprehensive and intelligent are his most remarkable
feature.' Olivier, needless to say, used his eyes to great effect and
said all the witty lines ('Martyrdom is the only way to achieve fame
without ability') most wittily. Effortlessly gallant, he was playful,
ironic, aristocratic, civilized and a bit of a dandy. He walked off with
the film.

The 1960s

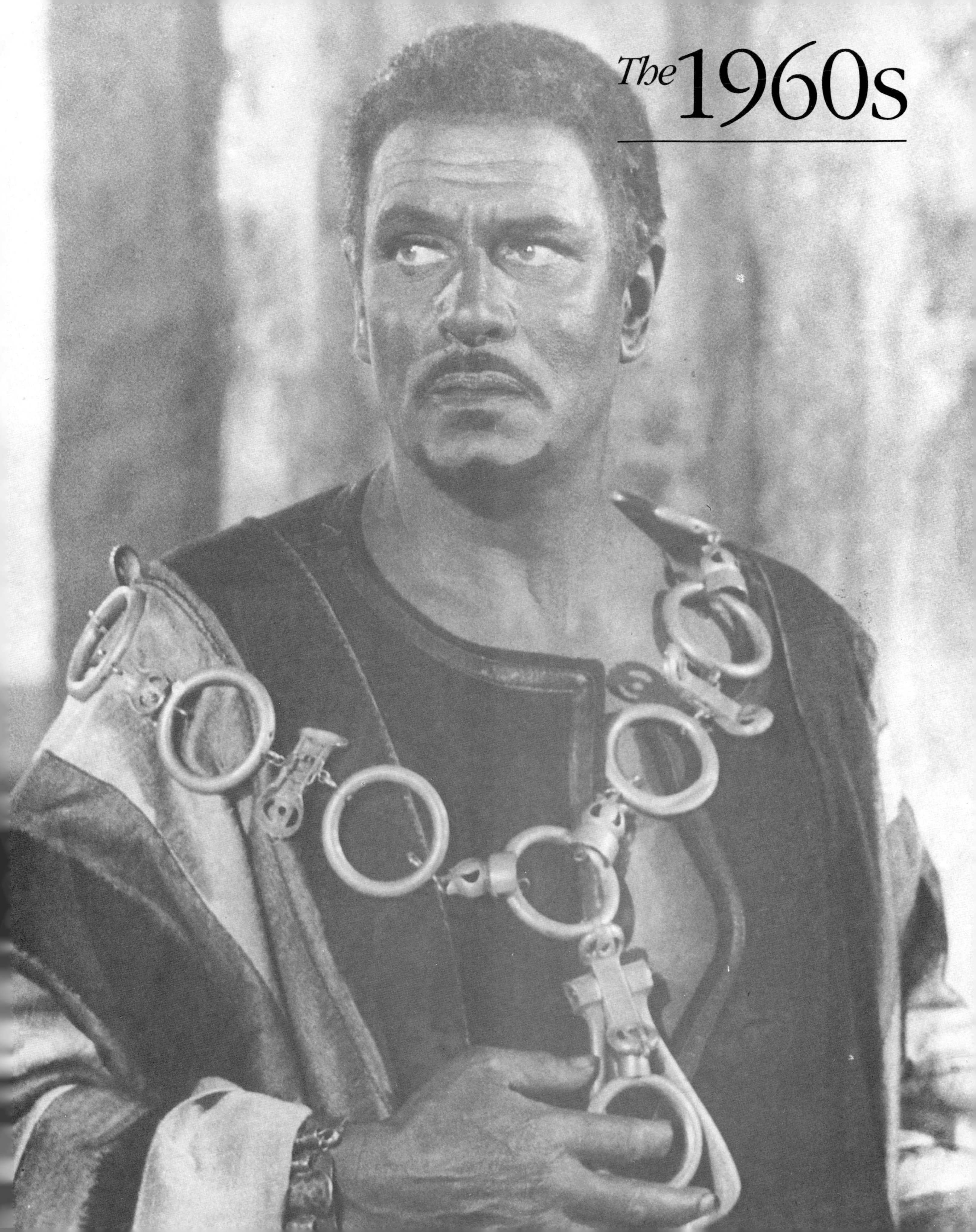

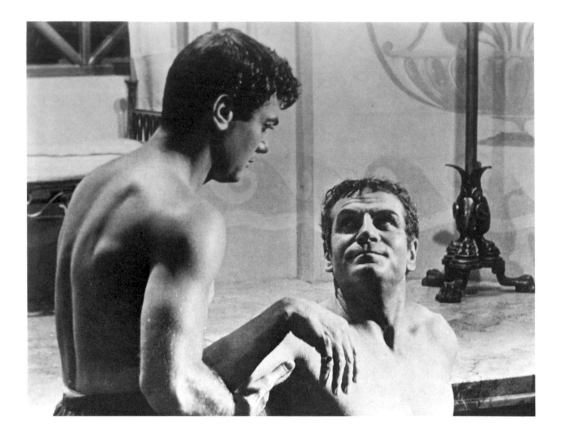

107 *Spartacus 1960*

Tony Curtis as the slave, Antonius, and Laurence Olivier as the Emperor Crassus in *Spartacus*, a film directed by Stanley Kubrick.

Since the American Legion of Decency insisted that a scene in which Crassus attempts to seduce his slave should be removed, Olivier was able only to hint at the general's homosexuality.

108 *Rhinoceros 1960*

Duncan Macrae, Michael Bates, Geoffrey Lumsden and Laurence Olivier in Eugene Ionesco's *Rhinoceros*, directed by Orson Welles at the Royal Court Theatre. The play transferred to the Strand Theatre.

Olivier played the one person who does not turn into a rhinoceros: a Chaplinesque little man, a clerk, worn out by work and drink, who refuses to join the herd.

109 *The Entertainer 1960*

Laurence Olivier as Archie Rice in the film version of John Osborne's
The Entertainer, directed by Tony Richardson.

110 *The Entertainer 1960*

Joan Plowright and Laurence Olivier in the film version of John
Osborne's *The Entertainer*.

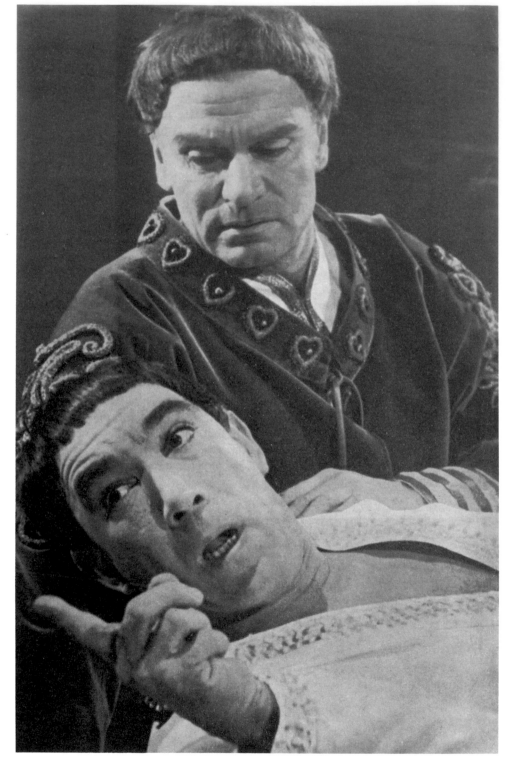

111 *Becket 1960*

Laurence Olivier as Becket and Anthony
Quinn as Henry II in Jean Anouilh's *Becket*,
directed by Peter Glenville at the St James's
Theatre, New York.
    Olivier played *both* leading roles, first the
prelate and then the king.

*Laurence Olivier, looking not only younger
than Henry V but even younger than Henry
II, turns a superbly knowing eye on his
nemesis as he refuses to accept his crony's
assurance that he will not be harmed. The
irony of his 'Poor Henry!' as Henry succeeds
in striking him down – forecasting the way
the game will really end in not too long a
time – is chilling in its clean, clear
knowledge.*
    *And this actor cannot be bested when it
comes to finding an occult and heart-lifting
inflection for a line that seems too pat ever
to be read freshly. He roars right into 'If I do
not defend my priests, who will?' and makes
the 'who will?' sound as though it were an
inspiration just sent him from heaven.*
    Walter Kerr *New York Herald Tribune*

112 *Becket 1961*

Laurence Olivier as Henry II and Arthur Kennedy as Becket in Jean Anouilh's *Becket*, directed by Peter Glenville at the Hudson Theatre, New York.

This is a Henry for whom you can weep as he writhes in almost epileptic spasm and screams and sobs in his anguished abandonment. And you weep because you have followed the course of his tragedy, seen the gay insouciance of his early confidence in Becket, his complete lack of understanding of his friend's character, his blind destruction of their relationship. Olivier, the master of the inflection, of the graceful implication, gives this Henry a tragic stature.

Judith Crist *New York Herald Tribune*

113 *The Power and the Glory 1961*

Julie Harris and Laurence Olivier in the television film version of Graham Greene's *The Power and the Glory*, directed by Marc Daniels.

   Olivier played the whiskey-priest, the last surviving priest in Mexico, who is on the run. George C. Scott played the police inspector who pursues him.

114 *Term of Trial 1962*

Simone Signoret and Laurence Olivier in *Term of Trial*, a film directed by Peter Glenville.

   Olivier played a shabby, meek, insignificant secondary-school teacher who is falsely accused of assault by one of his pupils. Sarah Miles played the pupil.

115 *The Broken Heart 1962*

Laurence Olivier as Bassanes, Rosemary Harris as Penthea and Keith Michell as Ithocles in John Ford's *The Broken Heart*, directed by Laurence Olivier at the Chichester Festival Theatre.

The play has a dark, brooding, Spartan power and Olivier tried hard in his production to give the plot the formal dignity of tragedy; but he was defeated by the characters who are not sufficiently interesting in their own right. The insanely and wrongfully jealous Bassanes, who drives his wife mad, even when acted with more seriousness than one might expect, still offered him few opportunities.

116 *Uncle Vanya 1962*

Joan Plowright as Sofya and Laurence Olivier as Astrov in Anton Chekhov's *Uncle Vanya*, directed by Laurence Olivier at the Chichester Festival Theatre. The production was revived in 1963 and then transferred to the National Theatre at the Old Vic.

Olivier's all-star revival, instantly recognized as one of the great Chekhovian productions of our time, put the Chichester Festival Theatre firmly on the theatrical map. The greatness of the production lay in the fine ensemble playing of the highly distinguished cast who caught perfectly the tragedy of stifled, cheated, wasted lives.

Olivier's Astrov (one of his favourite roles) was a study of feelings, blunted and coarsened by the banality of life in a provincial backwater. 'Life itself is tedious, stupid, dirty,' he says; and only too well aware that his and Vanya's situation is hopeless, he has retreated into apathy and drink. There was, in his performance, not only the hankering after a past which had gone for ever, but also the distress at the approach of 'hateful, detestable old age'.

117 *Semi-Detached 1962*

Laurence Olivier and Mona Washbourne in David Turner's *Semi-Detached*, directed by Tony Richardson at the Saville Theatre.

The first-night audience was clearly embarrassed, not only to find Olivier, balding and bespectacled, in a 'charabanc party' type comedy, but also to find that he was not good in it. David Turner's efforts to give the suburban vulgarity a veneer of social criticism did not come off at all and for Olivier, all too conscious that nobody liked him in the play, it was 'eighteen weeks of sheer torture'. The role of the Midlands salesman really needs a Midlands comedian; it had been created with great success by Leonard Rossiter at the Belgrade Theatre, Coventry.

118 *Uncle Vanya 1963*

Robert Lang as Yefim, Rosemary Harris as Ilyena, Joan Plowright as Sofya, Max Adrian as the Professor, Michael Redgrave as Vanya, Sybil Thorndike as the Nurse, Laurence Olivier as Astrov, Fay Compton as Maman and Lewis Casson as Waffles in the film version of the National Theatre's production of Chekhov's *Uncle Vanya*, directed by Laurence Olivier.

119 *The Recruiting Officer* 1963

Robert Stephens as Captain Plume and Laurence Olivier as Captain Brazen in George Farquhar's *The Recruiting Officer*, directed by William Gaskill at the National Theatre at the Old Vic.

This realistic and committed production (one of the most influential of the decade) emphasized that the comedy, based on Farquhar's own recruiting experiences, is far more than just a romp: it is, in fact, a social indictment of the age.

The officer class shares its beds with both men and women. Brazen and Plume are much addicted to kissing in public; indeed, on their first encounter, it was only after a very long embrace that Olivier's Brazen actually asked Robert Stephens' Plume his name.

Brazen, a bluff, ignorant, impertinent bore, comes of a long line of soldierly braggarts who have held the stage since Roman times. Olivier made much of this foolish, vain and extravagant creature ('Hot blood and guts are at your service') and he was very funny; though there was nothing to laugh at when he described how twenty horses had died under him in one day's battle.

120 *Othello 1964*

Frank Finlay as Iago and Laurence Olivier as Othello in Shakespeare's *Othello*, directed by John Dexter at the National Theatre at the Old Vic.

Kenneth Tynan, who had become the National Theatre's literary manager, amusingly suggested that the best way to celebrate Shakespeare's 400th birthday would be to act no Shakespeare at all in 1964. Fortunately he prevailed on Olivier, who did not think Othello was his part, to attempt the final Himalayan peak he had ignored for so long.

Olivier not only went to the gymnasium to get physically fit, he also deepened and darkened his voice. On the first night, he entered, barefoot, carrying a rose, the blackest white actor in living memory, romantic, magnetic and sexual.

The temptation scene was not unlike a bullfight: the questioning began quite tamely and then suddenly, there he was, on the rack, raging with jealousy, grovelling on the ground. The disintegration was truly terrifying. It was said that the transition from Christian nobility to barbaric fury was too quick; but that is the text. It was also said that his hysterical performance (bashing his head against the proscenium arch, weeping, 'O, Iago, the pity of it') was too theatrical; but that was its great strength. The acting had size. The scene ended electrifyingly with Othello ripping the large crucifix from his chest and forcing himself and Iago down on their knees to pray to some primitive god.

The production was an instant sell-out: there were queues round the block and standing ovations at every performance. In Moscow, where the company went in 1965, the applause continued for thirty-five minutes on the first night.

121 *Othello 1964*

Laurence Olivier as Othello.

In great tragic acting there is always a strong element of surprise. Othello, on the rack last night, was agonising in the sheer vehemence of his anguish, but it was the inventiveness of it above all, the sheer variety and range of the actor's art which made it an experience in the theatre altogether unforgettable by anyone who saw it. True it was the noble, wounded professional thrown out of kilter rather than the lumbering bull in Othello that was uppermost: the general self-broken, self-cashiered. 'Othello's occupation's gone.' We saw it go.
Philip Hope-Wallace *Guardian*

The power, passion, versimilitude and pathos of Sir Laurence's performance are things which will be spoken of with wonder for a long time to come. Sir Laurence speaks the line 'Not a jot' with a casual pain that is extremely moving; there is a tropical storm of energy in his 'Othello's occupation's gone'; with Emilia he is extraordinarily savage and intense; and to Maggie Smith's candid and rousing Desdemona tender and tormented.
Harold Hobson *The Sunday Times*

There is a kind of bad acting of which only a great actor is capable. I find Sir Laurence Olivier's Othello the most prodigious and perverse example of this in a decade.
Alan Brien *Sunday Telegraph*

122 *The Master Builder* 1964

Laurence Olivier as Halvard Solness and Maggie Smith as Hilde Wangel in Henrik Ibsen's *The Master Builder*, directed by Peter Wood at the National Theatre at the Old Vic.

When Olivier took over the role of the architect from Michael Redgrave, Maggie Smith and Joan Plowright alternated Hilde. *The Master Builder*, a self-portrait of Ibsen at sixty-one, could be seen, depending on which actress was playing, either as an old man's infatuation for a younger woman or a young woman's infatuation for an older man. The play's sexual excitement and booming blasphemy came across strongly. The fatal climb of the church spire (offstage) was given tremendous tension onstage by Celia Johnson playing Solness' wife.

Instead of taking his cue from the play's title, he has sought it in the character's past – a poor boy who fought his way to the top. This Solness is a thrusting vulgarian who has hoisted himself to middle class status but whose manners still compare coarsely with those of the doctor and his bloodlessly genteel wife. His fear of heights, later to take on cloudier significance, is thus firmly rooted in the fear of losing his precarious foothold in society.

The Times

In *Confessions of an Actor*, Olivier revealed that it was during a performance of *The Master Builder* at the Manchester Opera House in October 1964, on the pre-London tour, that his paralyzing stage-fright began; the stage-fright was to continue until April 1970.

123 *The Master Builder 1964*

Joan Plowright as Hilde Wangel and Laurence Olivier as Halvard
Solness in Henrik Ibsen's *The Master Builder*.

124 *Love for Love 1965*

Lyn Redgrave as Miss Prue and Laurence Olivier as Tattle in William Congreve's *Love for Love*, directed by Peter Wood at the National Theatre at the Old Vic. 'The half-witted beau, vain of his amours, yet valuing himself for secresie,' is seen here teaching 'a silly, awkward country girl' her catechism.

Olivier played Tattle, the male gossip, as a faded and somewhat effeminate fop. He was a delight when he sat down at the pianoforte to play and played nothing at all; he was even more delightful when he escaped from Miss Prue's bedroom window and tripped precariously along the top of the garden wall; and he was hilarious when he found himself married to Mrs Frail and, horrified, declared, 'I never liked anybody less in my life'. A supporting role became a major part.

125 *Othello 1965*

Laurence Olivier as Othello and Maggie Smith as Desdemona in the film version of John Dexter's National Theatre production of Shakespeare's *Othello*, directed by Stuart Burge.

Olivier was doing exactly what he had done at the Old Vic but the camera wasn't able to capture it. Clearly it would have been wiser to adapt to the new medium, rather than merely repeat his stage performance. Though there are moments (notably in the temptation scene, the hysterical bullying of Desdemona, and in the actual *crime passionel*) which are as wonderful as they always were, the big set pieces are frankly too theatrical for comfort and the very size of the original conception plays against the actor. He seems to be acting in an empty theatre. As a film, *Othello* is dreary; and as a record, it may, in the long run, do a disservice to Olivier's reputation. Certainly it does not do justice to his original performance.

126 *Khartoum 1966*

Laurence Olivier as the Mahdi and Charlton Heston as General
Gordon in *Khartoum*, a film directed by Basil Dearden.

127 *A Flea in her Ear* 1967

Peter Cellier and Laurence Olivier in Georges Feydeau's farce, *A Flea in her Ear*, directed by Jacques Charon. Olivier played Plucheux, the butler, on the National Theatre's tour of Canada.

128 *The Dance of Death 1967*

Robert Stephens as Kurt, Laurence Olivier as Edgar and Geraldine McEwan as Alice in August Strindberg's *The Dance of Death*, directed by Glen Byam Shaw at the National Theatre at the Old Vic.

The line of demarcation between melodrama and farce can be unnervingly thin in Strindberg's play and Edgar's remark that he very nearly pushed his wife off the pier may be funny or not, depending on the night one goes. Olivier was splendid in his triumph over his wife and her lover; he seized and exploited his opportunities, the voice becoming more and more military, more and more clipped – 'I'm not dead yet, I can tell you!'

He got a round of applause for the ironic way he tapped the French window when he came on, while at the beginning of the fourth scene in the first act, he said nothing and held the audience absolutely hushed by sheer presence. His Captain Edgar was coarse and arrogant; his hatred, ferocious. There were twenty years of marital vindictiveness stored in that close-cropped Prussian head.

As the husband, Laurence Olivier, a misanthropic tyrant despising life almost as much as he does his wife, gives a superb performance of selfish, bullying grandeur.

Milton Shulman *Evening Standard*

Olivier's Edgar is a masterly creation of snarling venom, vulgarity and self-pity shot through with shafts of alarming politeness that indicate yet nastier behaviour in the offing.

Jeremy Kingston *Punch*

This is a masterpiece. It contains many aspects – bullying martinet, convivial vulgarian, twinkling old gentleman – but underlying them all is the rancour of a man who has been passed over.

Irving Wardle *The Times*

129 *The Shoes of the Fisherman 1968*

Laurence Olivier as the Russian Premier, Anthony Quinn as the Pope and Burt Kwouk as Peng in the film version of Morris West's *The Shoes of the Fisherman*, directed by Michael Anderson.

130 *Oh! What A Lovely War 1969*

Isabel Dean and Laurence Olivier in the film version of Joan Littlewood and Charles Hilton's *Oh! What A Lovely War*, directed by Richard Attenborough. Olivier played a sozzled, tangoing Field Marshal Sir John French.

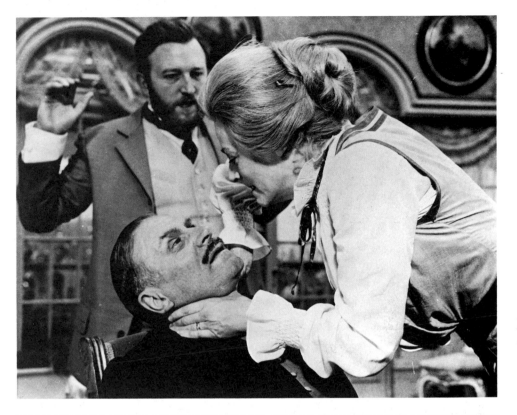

131 *The Battle of Britain* 1969

Laurence Olivier as Air Chief Marshal Sir Hugh Dowding, Commander-in-Chief of Fighter Command, in *The Battle of Britain*, a film directed by Guy Hamilton.

132 *The Dance of Death* 1969

Robert Lang as Kurt, Laurence Olivier as Edgar and Geraldine McEwan as Alice in the film version of the Glen Byam Shaw National Theatre production of August Strindberg's *The Dance of Death*, directed by David Giles.

133 *Home and Beauty* 1969

Laurence Olivier, Robert Lang and Geraldine McEwan in W. Somerset Maugham's *Home and Beauty*, directed by Frank Dunlop at the National Theatre at the Old Vic.

In preparation for Shylock, Olivier decided to ease himself back into the theatre in a cameo part. The programme billed him as Walter Plinge, a well-known theatrical device to hide the true identity of the actor. Olivier played Mr A.B. Raham, one of the busiest divorce solicitors in London, a role in Somerset Maugham's best cynical vein.

134 *David Copperfield 1969*

Richard Attenborough as the wooden-legged Mr Tungay and
Laurence Olivier as the ignorant and ferocious schoolmaster, Mr
Creakle, in the film version of Charles Dickens' *David Copperfield*,
directed by Delbert Mann.

*I should think there never can have been a man who enjoyed his
profession more than Mr. Creakle did. He had a delight in cutting at
the boys, which was like the satisfaction of a craving appetite. I am
confident that he couldn't resist a chubby boy, especially; that there
was a fascination in such a subject, which made him restless in his
mind, until he had scored and marked him for the day.*

Charles Dickens

Olivier, making the briefest of brief appearances, enjoyed the
horrors of school at Salem House hugely. Alexander Walker, critic
for the *Evening Standard*, said he and Richard Attenborough were 'a
perfect Dickensian double act'.

The 1970s

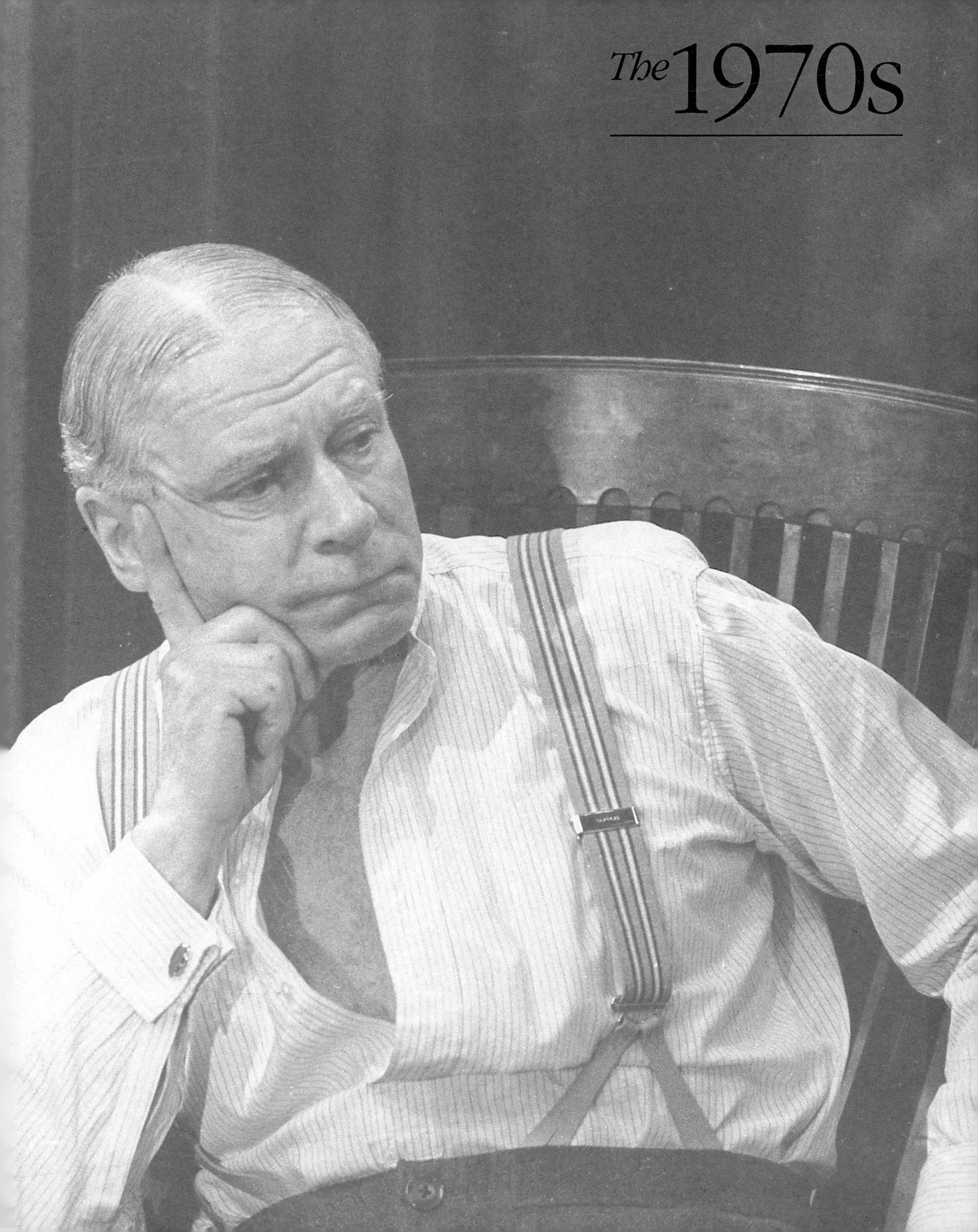

135 *Three Sisters 1970*

Laurence Olivier as the army doctor, Chebutikin, in the film version of his National Theatre production of Anton Chekhov's *Three Sisters*, which he also directed.

136 *The Merchant of Venice 1970*

Laurence Olivier as Shylock and Joan Plowright as Portia in Shakespeare's *The Merchant of Venice*, directed by Jonathan Miller at the National Theatre at the Old Vic.

Jonathan Miller set the play in the late nineteenth century, where the action could be seen within the context of the rising middle classes. The most original touch of all was to play the trial scene in a private courtroom, where the matter of the pound of flesh could be discussed over the table.

Olivier came up with something entirely new, which owed nothing to the stereotype Jews of the past. He was neither a conventional villain, nor a tragic figure; rather he was the vulgar nouveau riche on the make, anxious to be accepted by the Christian fraternity and all the more bitter that he was not. Though this self-made man was never likeable and his insistence on the bond was as unpleasant as it always is, the dénouement was made even more upsetting, in this production, by Gratiano's gross insensitivity and Bassanio's obvious embarrassment. Shylock's collapse was delayed until he was in the wings; Olivier did not cry until he was offstage.

At one performance, the trial scene was interrupted by a hysterical woman in the upper circle, who asked Olivier why he had put on this terrible play and hadn't the Jews already suffered enough under the Nazis. When she had been removed, the scene continued, moving inexorably to the line when Antonio insists that Shylock becomes a Christian. The audience felt acutely uncomfortable.

137 *Long Day's Journey Into Night 1971*

Laurence Olivier as James Tyrone and Constance Cummings as Mary Cavan Tyrone in Eugene O'Neill's *Long Day's Journey Into Night*, directed by Michael Blakemore at the New Theatre.

O'Neill's painfully autobiographical play, written in blood and tears, is an act of expiation: four hours of unrelenting recriminations in which the knife goes deeply into the same wound, over and over again. Olivier, as the famous actor, trapped and ruined by his own commercial success, caught all the bitterness, anger and self-pity; he was particularly impressive when talking about his childhood and remembering the time when he and his mother were so poor that they did not have enough to eat.

One thing I would emphasize among his many talents and attributes would be his generosity to other players. He always exercises great concentration on the parts he is playing but never to the exclusion of the other people in the cast. He is always alert and sympathetic to the other actors. This is not true of all great performers.

Constance Cummings

138 *Lady Caroline Lamb* *1972*

Laurence Olivier as the Duke of Wellington and Sarah Miles as
Caroline Lamb in *Lady Caroline Lamb,* a film written and directed by
Robert Bolt. Caroline Lamb attempts to seduce the Duke in the hope
of furthering the career of her husband, Lord Melbourne.

139 *Long Day's Journey Into Night* 1972

The Tyrone family: Ronald Pickup as Edmund, Denis Quilley as Jamie, Laurence Olivier as James and Constance Cummings as Mary in the television version of Michael Blakemore's National Theatre production of Eugene O'Neill's *Long Day's Journey Into Night*, directed by Peter Wood.

'An infinite capacity for taking pains'? '90 per cent perspiration, 10 per cent inspiration'? He is the living embodiment of the truth of both these popular attempts to define genius.

At rehearsal I never saw anyone work so hard: chipping away with endless patience and determination at that great granite rock of a play until he found and released the form he was looking for inside it. And in performances sometimes so tired (he was after all running the National Theatre by day and playing this monstrous role every night) that he would fall asleep during a one-minute break between scenes and I would have to wake him for our entrance.

When young actors ask me what qualities are most needed for success in the theatre I think of him and reply 'hard graft'.

Denis Quilley

140 *Saturday, Sunday, Monday 1973*

Joan Plowright and Laurence Olivier in Eduardo de Filippo's *Saturday, Sunday, Monday,* a slice of Neapolitan family life, directed by Franco Zeffirelli at the National Theatre at the Old Vic.

Olivier had the smallest of roles: the mischievous grandfather whose lifelong obsession with hats (he was a hatter) leads him to seize any that their owners might unwisely have left lying around and stretch and pummel them into the most extraordinary shapes. It was a scene-stealing cameo.

141 *The Merchant of Venice 1973*

Laurence Olivier as Shylock in the television version of the National Theatre production of Shakespeare's *The Merchant of Venice*, directed by Jonathan Miller.

142 *The Merchant of Venice 1973*

Joan Plowright as Portia, Michael Jayston as Gratiano, Jeremy Brett as Bassanio, Benjamin Whitrow as the Duke of Venice and Laurence Olivier as Shylock in the television version of the National Theatre production of Shakespeare's *The Merchant of Venice*.

Several memories spring to mind when I think of working with Laurence Olivier. One is more detailed than the other. The first memory is an impression or an atmosphere he creates as an actor, as opposed to any specific details of his performance. He generates what actors often enviously refer to as an air of danger. The notion of the dangerous actor is one of the myths that is often talked about in the profession and Laurence Olivier exemplifies it more vividly perhaps, and more comprehensively, than almost any other performer I have watched or with whom I have worked. It captivates and fascinates those who are on stage with him as much as the people who are watching him in the audience. It is the uneasy and above all tantalizing impression that you cannot say for certain what he is going to do next. He gives the impression that there are almost bottomless reserves of energy and determination from which he can draw to realize unexpected and, in many cases, quite alarming inflections or gestures. The result is that he keeps both the stage and the auditorium in a state of delighted vigilance, lending a peculiar, risky vitality to an event which might otherwise seem quite commonplace and predictable. Thinking about this by hindsight, I have often been irresistibly reminded of a werewolf or vampire. He is somebody who can enter a scene with the deceptive demeanour of someone quite inconspicuous and ordinary, but who can, at any moment, transfer himself into something quite alarming and ferocious.

He preserves this spectacular anonymity when he is off-stage. On the few occasions I have accompanied him in public, thinking that we would be besieged by glances and whispers of recognition, I was startled, and perhaps disappointed, to find that he had effortlessly assumed a protective coloration and that he was no more recognizable than a bank manager or an insurance clerk. It is from this 'hide' that he often makes his most spectacular sallies when he is on the stage; and audiences await them with the expectant hush of children watching a conjurer who invariably fulfils his promise of performing a dangerous and perhaps impossible feat of prestidigitation. He is the only actor I know who is capable of hypnotizing and even terrorizing an audience with his back turned. Like a toreador, confident of his lethal skill, Olivier can indolently avert his gaze and excite his public in the knowledge that he will blaze with some unexpected fierceness on his return.

But he also has an almost obsessional mastery of physical detail and this often leads him in rehearsal to what seems like a pedantic interest in the technical possibilites of certain props. When I was working on The Merchant of Venice in 1969, he showed an almost child-like pleasure in a strangely curved and piebald walking stick which Julia Oman had found for him. He fondled the ebony knob and took a delicate delight in the way in which he could poise the stick and twirl it on its brass ferrule. He learned to swing it with a deadly nonchalance across his broad shoulders and I remember the envious looks of some of the younger actors who tried to emulate this elegant sword-play. He had an almost supernatural mastery of his top hat – a fastidious familiarity with its brim and crown. And I can still remember watching the meticulous care with which he handled the brief-case we provided for him in the trial scene. Each memory delivers another one as I recall the physical creativity of this matchless performer.

Jonathan Miller

143 *The Party* 1973

Gillian Barge, Gawn Grainger and Laurence Olivier in Trevor Griffiths' *The Party*, directed by John Dexter at the National Theatre at the Old Vic.

It had been hoped (wishful thinking, really) that Olivier might make his farewell in *King Lear*; instead he bowed out of the National Theatre playing an elderly Glaswegian Trotskyite, who has an eighteen-minute monologue on the futility of a revolutionary party formed without the participation of the working classes. His brow-mopping harangue, bursting with rage and irony – 'You enjoy biting the hand that feeds you, but you will never bite it off' – had a passionate conviction. The highlight, however, was the moment when Olivier remembered his meeting with Trotsky.

144 *Love Among the Ruins* 1975

Katharine Hepburn and Laurence Olivier in the television film version of Angela Thirkell's *Love Among the Ruins*, directed by George Cukor. Olivier played a barrister, who has been in love with his client for forty years.

What can one say about Larry? Sweet . . . wicked . . . fascinating . . . and right up on top of the ladder . . . where he began and will end . . . dropped there by an angel and he can fly . . . so he won't fall off.
Katharine Hepburn

145 *The Seven-Per-Cent Solution* 1976

Laurence Olivier as Professor Moriarty in *The Seven-Per-Cent Solution*, a film directed by Herbert Ross.

Nicholas Meyer's novel takes Moriarty, Conan Doyle's master criminal, and turns him into a nervous wreck of an old mathematics professor, who was once Holmes' tutor and has never done him any harm. Olivier gave a witty and inventive performance. Nicol Williamson played the deluded, drug-addicted, paranoid Holmes.

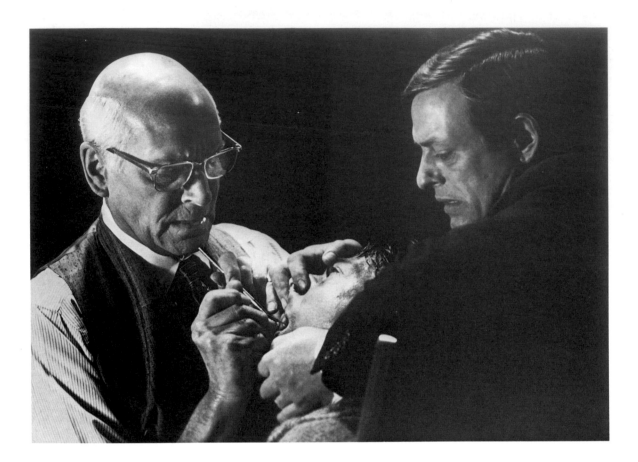

146 *Marathon Man 1976*

Laurence Olivier, Dustin Hoffman and Richard Bright in *Marathon Man*, a film directed by John Schlesinger.

Olivier played a Nazi war criminal, a former prison-camp doctor and one of the world's most wanted men. He has a fortune in gold fillings stacked away in a New York bank vault and comes out of hiding to collect his loot. Here he is seen giving Dustin Hoffman an unforgettable lesson in dentistry.

147 *The Collection 1976*

Laurence Olivier as Harry Kane in Harold Pinter's television play, *The Collection*, directed by Michael Apted.

There are two marriages on the rocks: one heterosexual, the other homosexual. Olivier played the dress designer whose boyfriend may or may not have slept with somebody else's wife. The cast also included Malcolm McDowell as the boyfriend and Helen Mirren and Alan Bates as the wife and her husband.

A psychological war in which nobody, least of all Harold Pinter, is admitting *anything*, was acted out with economy and wit. The studied, menacing ambiguity had elegance.

148 *Cat on a Hot Tin Roof 1976*

Robert Wagner as Brick and Laurence Olivier as Big Daddy in the television production of Tennessee Williams' *Cat on a Hot Tin Roof*, directed by Robert Moore.

Big Daddy is dying of cancer and doesn't know it; his son is a homosexual and won't admit it. The big scene they share is one of the most powerful in twentieth-century drama. The television production, unwisely mixing American and English actors, turned Tennessee Williams into a glossy, slushy Hollywood movie; and the script seemed terrible. The lacerating self-disgust and over-heated Southern hysterics worked best on the small screen when Maureen Stapleton, playing Big Mama, was around.

149 *Jesus of Nazareth 1977*

Robert Powell as Jesus and Laurence Olivier as Nicodemus in *Jesus of Nazareth*, a film made for television, directed by Franco Zeffirelli.

150 *A Bridge Too Far 1977*

Liv Ullmann and Laurence Olivier in *A Bridge Too Far*, the story of Arnhem, a film directed by Richard Attenborough. Olivier played a Dutch doctor, who pleads with the Germans for a cease-fire in order to remove the wounded and bury the dead.

◁ 151 *The Betsy 1978*

Laurence Olivier as the founder of a giant motor corporation in Harold Robbins' *The Betsy*, a film directed by Daniel Petrie.

152 *Come Back, Little Sheba 1978*

Laurence Olivier as Doc Delaney, in William Inge's *Come Back, Little Sheba*, directed for television by Silvio Narizzano.

Olivier, playing the alcoholic Doc, unhappily married to a slovenly woman, had a fine scene when, having been off the bottle for a year, he suddenly and frighteningly went berserk and had to be taken back to the hospital where the drunks and lunatics were housed in the same ward.

153 *Daphne Laureola* 1978

Clive Arrindell and Laurence Olivier in the television production of
James Bridie's *Daphne Laureola*, directed by Waris Hussein.

Olivier had presented Edith Evans in James Bridie's play in the
West End in 1949. In 1978 he revived it on television for his wife,
Joan Plowright; but it was not until he himself appeared in the small
but important role of the seventy-eight-year-old husband that the
play became worth watching.

First there was an amusing little scene when Sir Joseph warned off
the adoring Marchbanks-like student; and then there was another
telling little scene when he told his wife that he had never regretted
marrying her. For many viewers the scene gained an added
poignancy because they knew the actors were married in real life
and because they knew that Olivier had been very ill.

Lady Pitts	*What's the matter with you?*
Sir Joseph	*Death, my dear. The first natural thing that has happened to me in half a century.*
Lady Pitts	*Joe, don't go! I need you.*

154 *The Boys from Brazil 1978*

Gregory Peck, Jeremy Black and Laurence Olivier in the film version of Ira Levin's *The Boys from Brazil*, a thriller about a Nazi war criminal cloning little Hitlers all over the world, directed by Franklin J. Schaffner. Olivier played a famous Nazi-hunter, based on the real-life Nazi-hunter, Simon Wiesenthal.

155 *Saturday, Sunday, Monday 1978*

John Duttine and Laurence Olivier in the television production of Eduardo de Filippo's *Saturday, Sunday, Monday*, directed by Allan Bridges. Olivier repeated his role of the grandfather.

156 *A Little Romance 1979*

Laurence Olivier in *A Little Romance*, a film directed by George Roy Hill. He played an elderly French pickpocket who befriends two teenage sweethearts and is then accused of kidnapping them.

157 *Dracula 1979*

Frank Langella as Count Dracula and Laurence Olivier as Professor
Van Helsing in *Dracula*, a film directed by John Badham.

158 *The Jazz Singer* 1980

Laurence Olivier and Neil Diamond in *The Jazz Singer*, a re-make of the 1927 Al Jolson film, directed by Richard Fleischer. Olivier played a Jewish cantor whose son wants to be in show business.

159 *Clash of the Titans* 1981

Laurence Olivier as Zeus in *Clash of the Titans*, a film directed by Desmond David.

◁ 160 *Brideshead Revisited* 1981

Laurence Olivier and Diana Quick in Evelyn Waugh's *Brideshead Revisited*, directed for television by Charles Sturridge and Michael Lindsay-Hogg. Olivier played the dying Lord Marchmain, wearing himself out with the struggle to live. It was an urbane performance, suggesting hidden strengths beneath the surface calm.

161 *A Voyage Round My Father* 1982

Elizabeth Sellars, Laurence Olivier and Alan Cox in the television production of John Mortimer's *A Voyage Round My Father*, directed by Alvin Rakoff.

Olivier played the famous blind barrister, a master of rhetoric, both in the courtroom and in his home. Making great play with his eyes, blind though they were, he caught the egotism, selfishness and affectation of the man perfectly. Perhaps the most delightful moment was on the train when, to the consternation of the other commuters, he insisted on his wife reading out to him all the intimate details of a divorce case and laughed so much that he cried.

When Laurence Olivier said he'd do A Voyage Round My Father *he said it's no good playing this character for sympathy. Then I not only knew he would be right, but that he would get all the sympathy in the world.*

John Mortimer

162 *King Lear 1983*

Diana Rigg as Goneril, Leo McKern as Gloucester and Laurence Olivier as Lear in the television production of Shakespeare's *King Lear*, directed by Michael Elliott.

The most original touch was, as it had been at the Old Vic all those years ago, to play the abdication scene as a kindly, silly old man's joke – a joke into which only Diana Rigg's Goneril was willing to enter wholeheartedly. Olivier was at his most moving in the quieter passages, as when he prayed to be sane or in his scene with the blinded Gloucester.

163 *A Talent for Murder 1983*

Angela Lansbury as a writer of detective fiction and Laurence Olivier
as her doctor in *A Talent for Murder*, a television comedy thriller by
Jerome Choderov and Norman Panama, directed by Alvin Rakoff.

164 *Mr Halpern and Mr Johnson 1984*

Jackie Gleason and Laurence Olivier in Lionel Goldstein's television
play, *Mr Halpern and Mr Johnson*, directed by Alvin Rakoff.

Olivier played Mr Halpern, the elderly Jewish widower, who
discovers for the first time that his wife has had a platonic
relationship with a rich American accountant all his married life.

165 *The Bounty 1984*

Laurence Olivier as Admiral Hood and Anthony Hopkins as Captain
Bligh in *The Bounty*, a film directed by Roger Donaldson. Hood
presided over the court martial of Captain Bligh. Mel Gibson played
Mr Christian.

166 *The Ebony Tower 1984*

Laurence Olivier as an English painter in John Fowles' *The Ebony
Tower*, directed for television by Robert Knights.

When the painter said, 'You can't have any art without danger',
Olivier could easily have been talking about himself. It is an
aphorism which has informed his whole acting career.

Never more vulnerable than when he was being most aggressive,
Olivier's selfish old man was no monster at all but rather an
extremely tame dragon, frightened that a priggish and modern St
George would, misguidedly, rob him of his lady. He was always
totally believable as a painter and the vulnerability was acted with
great sensitivity and without sentimentality.

167 *Wagner 1985*

Ralph Richardson, Laurence Olivier and John Gielgud as three ministers at the court of Ludwig II in *Wagner*, a film made for television, directed by Tony Palmer. Richard Burton played Wagner.

168 *The Jigsaw Man 1985*

Susan George, Laurence Olivier and Michael Caine (on the stretcher) in *The Jigsaw Man*, a film directed by Terence Young. Olivier played the Director General of the British Secret Service.

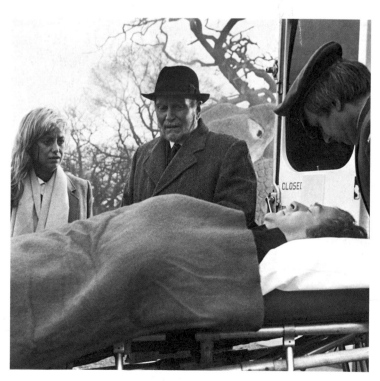

169 *Wild Geese II   1985*

Laurence Olivier as Rudolph Hess in *Wild Geese II*, directed by Peter Hunt. The film is about an attempt to spring Hess from Spandau prison.

Chronology

Theatre · Films · Television
Director · Management · Radio
Awards and Honours

Index
Acknowledgments

Chronology

Theatre

Date	Play	Role	Writer	Director	Theatre
All Saints Church Choir School 1916-21					
1917					
	Julius Caesar	Brutus	William Shakespeare	Geoffrey Heald	
	Twelfth Night	Maria	William Shakespeare	Geoffrey Heald	
1920					
	The Taming of the Shrew	Katharine	William Shakespeare	Geoffrey Heald	
1922 Apr	The Taming of the Shrew	Katharine	William Shakespeare	Geoffrey Heald	Memorial, Stratford-upon-Avon
St Edward's School 1921-24					
1923	A Midsummer Night's Dream	Puck	William Shakespeare	W.H.A. Cowell	
Central School of Speech Training and Dramatic Art 1924					
1924 Feb	Macbeth	Lennox and ASM	William Shakespeare	Beatrice Wilson	St Christopher, Letchworth
Nov	Byron	Suliot Officer	Alice Law	Henry Oscar	Century
1925 Jan	Through the Crack	ASM and understudy	Algernon Blackwood	Edith Craig	St Christopher, Letchworth
Feb	Henry IV Part II	Master Snare and Thomas of Clarence	William Shakespeare	L.E. Berman	Regent
	Unfailing Instinct	Armand St Cyr	Julian Frank	Julian Frank	Hippodrome, Brighton and tour
	The Ghost Train	Policeman	Arnold Ridley	Julian Frank	Hippodrome, Brighton and tour
Lena Ashwell Players: Century Theatre and tour of London 1925					
1925 Oct	The Tempest	Antonio	William Shakespeare	Lena Ashwell	
Oct	Julius Caesar	Flavius	William Shakespeare	Lena Ashwell	
1925 Dec	Henry VIII	First Serving Man	William Shakespeare	Lewis Casson	Empire
1926 Mar	The Cenci	Servant to Orsino	Percy Bysshe Shelley	Lewis Casson	Empire
Apr	The Marvellous History of Saint Bernard	Minstrel	Henri Ghéon translated by Barry Jackson	A.E. Filmer	Kingsway
	The Barber and the Cow	small part	D.T. Davies	H.K. Ayliff	Clacton
	The Farmer's Wife	Richard Coaker	Eden Phillpott	H.K. Ayliff	Touring
Birmingham Repertory Theatre 1926-1927					
1926 Dec	The Farmer's Wife	Richard Coaker	Eden Phillpott	H.K. Ayliff	
1927 Jan	Something To Talk About	Guy Sydney	Eden Phillpott	W.G. Fay	
Jan	The Well of the Saints	Mat Simon	J.M. Synge	W.G. Fay	
Feb	The Third Finger	Tom Hardcastle	R.R. Whittaker	W.G. Fay	
Feb	The Mannoch Family	Peter Mannoch	M. McClymond	W.G. Fay	
Mar	The Comedian	Walk on	Henri Ghéon adapted by Alan Bland	W.G. Fay	
Apr	Uncle Vanya	Vanya	Anton Chekhov translated by Constance Garnett	W.G. Fay	

Date	Play	Role	Writer	Director	Theatre
Birmingham Repertory Theatre	**1926-1927**				
1927					
Apr	All's Well That Ends Well	Parolles	William Shakespeare	W.G. Fay	
Apr	The Pleasure Garden	Young Man	Beatrice Mayor	W.G. Fay	
May	She Stoops To Conquer	Tony Lumpkin	Oliver Goldsmith	W.G. Fay	
Jun	Quality Street	Ensign Blades	J.M. Barrie	W.G. Fay	
Sep	Bird in Hand	Gerald Arnwood	John Drinkwater	John Drinkwater	
Sep	Advertising April	Mervyn Jones	Herbert Farjeon and Horace Horsnell	W.G. Fay	
Oct	The Silver Box	Jack Barthwick	John Galsworthy	W.G. Fay	
Oct	The Adding Machine	Young Man	Elmer Rice	W.G. Fay	
Nov	Aren't Women Wonderful?	Ben Hawley	Harris Dean	W.G. Fay	
Dec	The Road to Ruin	Mr Milford	Thomas Holcroft	W.G. Fay	
Court Theatre	**1928**				
1928					
Jan	The Adding Machine	Young Man	Elmer Rice	W.G. Fay	
Jan	Macbeth	Malcolm	William Shakespeare	H.K. Ayliff	
Mar	Back to Methuselah	Martellus	Bernard Shaw	H.K. Ayliff	
Apr	Harold	Harold	Alfred, Lord Tennyson	H.K. Ayliff	
Apr	The Taming of the Shrew	A Lord	William Shakespeare	H.K. Ayliff	
1928					
Jun	Bird in Hand	Gerald Arnwood	John Drinkwater	John Drinkwater	Royalty
Nov	The Dark Path	Graham Birley	Evan John	Evan John	Royalty
Dec	Journey's End	Captain Stanhope	R.C. Sherriff	James Whale	Apollo (Stage Society)
1929					
Jan	Beau Geste	Beau	Basil Dean and Charlton Mann's adaptation of P.C. Wren	Basil Dean	His Majesty's
Mar	The Circle of Chalk	Prince Pao	Klabund adapted by James Laver	Basil Dean	New
Apr	Paris Bound	Richard Parish	Philip Barry	Arthur Hopkins	Lyric
Jun	The Stranger Within	John Hardy	Crane Wilbur	Reginald Bach	Garrick
Sep	Murder on the Second Floor	Hugh Bromilow	Frank Vosper	William Mollison	Eltinge, New York
Dec	The Last Enemy	Jerry Warrender	Frank Harvey	Tom Walls	Fortune
1930					
Mar	After All	Ralph	John van Druten	Auriol Lee	Arts
Sep	Private Lives	Victor Prynne	Noël Coward	Noël Coward	Phoenix
1931					
Jan	Private Lives	Victor Prynne	Noël Coward	Noël Coward	Times Square, New York
1933					
Apr	The Rats of Norway	Steven Beringer	Keith Winter	Raymond Massey	Playhouse
Oct	The Green Bay Tree	Julian Dulcimer	Mordaunt Shairp	Jed Harris	Cort, New York
1934					
Apr	Biography	Richard Kurt	S.N. Behrman	Noël Coward	Globe
Jun	Queen of Scots	Bothwell	Gordon Daviot	John Gielgud	New
Oct	Theatre Royal	Anthony Cavendish	Edna Ferber and George S. Kaufman	Noël Coward	Lyric
1935					
Mar	Ringmaster	Peter Hammond	Keith Winter	Raymond Massey	Shaftesbury
May	Golden Arrow	Richard Harben	Sylvia Thompson and Victor Cunard	Laurence Olivier	Whitehall
Oct	Romeo and Juliet	Romeo	William Shakespeare	John Gielgud	New
Nov	Romeo and Juliet	Mercutio	William Shakespeare	John Gielgud	New
1936					
May	Bees on the Boatdeck	Robert Patch	J.B. Priestley	Laurence Olivier and Ralph Richardson	Lyric

Date	Play	Role	Writer	Director	Theatre

Old Vic Company at the Old Vic Theatre   1937-1938

1937

Jan	Hamlet	Hamlet	William Shakespeare	Tyrone Guthrie	
Feb	Twelfth Night	Sir Toby Belch	William Shakespeare	Tyrone Guthrie	
Apr	Henry V	Henry	William Shakespeare	Tyrone Guthrie	
Jun	Hamlet	Hamlet	William Shakespeare	Tyrone Guthrie	Elsinore, Denmark
Nov	Macbeth	Macbeth	William Shakespeare	Michel St Denis	(also at New)

1938

Feb	Othello	Iago	William Shakespeare	Tyrone Guthrie	
Mar	The King of Nowhere	Vivaldi	James Bridie	Tyrone Guthrie	
Apr	Coriolanus	Coriolanus	William Shakespeare	Lewis Casson	

New York   1939-1940

1939

Apr	No Time for Comedy	Gaylord Easterbrook	S.N. Behrman	Guthrie McClintic	Ethel Barrymore

1940

May	Romeo and Juliet	Romeo	William Shakespeare	Laurence Olivier	51st Street

The Old Vic Company at the New Theatre   1944-1946

1944

Aug	Peer Gynt	Button-Moulder	Henrik Ibsen adapted by Norman Ginsburg	Tyrone Guthrie and Robert Helpmann	
Sep	Arms and the Man	Sergius Saranoff	Bernard Shaw	John Burrell	
Sep	Richard III	Gloucester	William Shakespeare	John Burrell	

1945

Jan	Uncle Vanya	Astrov	Anton Chekhov translated by Constance Garnett	John Burrell	
Sep	Henry IV Part I	Hotspur	William Shakespeare	John Burrell	
Oct	Henry IV Part II	Shallow	William Shakespeare	John Burrell	
Oct	Oedipus Rex	Oedipus	Sophocles translated by W.B. Yeats	Michel St Denis	
Oct	The Critic	Mr Puff	Richard Brinsley Sheridan	Miles Malleson	

1946

Sep	King Lear	Lear	William Shakespeare	Laurence Olivier	

The company went to the Comédie Française in Paris, and Antwerp, Ghent, Bruges in 1945, and New York in 1946.

The Old Vic Company tour Australia and New Zealand   1948

1948

Mar–	Richard III	Gloucester	William Shakespeare	John Burrell	
Oct	The School for Scandal	Sir Peter Teazle	Richard Brinsley Sheridan	Laurence Olivier	
	The Skin of Our Teeth	Mr Antrobus	Thornton Wilder	Laurence Olivier	

The company went to Perth, Adelaide, Melbourne, Hobart, Sydney, Brisbane, Auckland, Christchurch, Dunedin, Wellington.

The Old Vic Company at the New Theatre   1949

1949

Jan	Richard III	Gloucester	William Shakespeare	John Burrell	
Jan	The School for Scandal	Sir Peter Teazle	Richard Brinsley Sheridan	Laurence Olivier	
Jan	Antigone	Chorus	Jean Anouilh translated by Lewis Galantière	Laurence Olivier	

1950

Jan	Venus Observed	Duke of Altair	Christopher Fry	Laurence Olivier	St James's

1951

May	Caesar and Cleopatra	Caesar	Bernard Shaw	Michael Benthall	St James's
May	Antony and Cleopatra	Antony	William Shakespeare	Michael Benthall	St James's
Dec	Caesar and Cleopatra	Caesar	Bernard Shaw	Michael Benthall	Ziegfeld, New York
Dec	Antony and Cleopatra	Antony	William Shakespeare	Michael Benthall	Ziegfeld, New York

1953

Nov	The Sleeping Prince	Grand Duke	Terence Rattigan	Laurence Olivier	Phoenix

Theatre

DATE	PLAY	ROLE	WRITER	DIRECTOR	THEATRE

Memorial Theatre, Stratford-upon-Avon   1955

1955					
Apr	Twelfth Night	Malvolio	William Shakespeare	John Gielgud	
Jun	Macbeth	Macbeth	William Shakespeare	Glen Byam Shaw	
Aug	Titus Andronicus	Titus	William Shakespeare	Peter Brook	
1957					
Apr	The Entertainer	Archie Rice	John Osborne	Tony Richardson	Royal Court

Memorial Theatre European Tour   1957

1957					
May-Jun	Titus Andronicus	Titus	William Shakespeare	Peter Brook	

The company went to Paris, Venice, Vienna, Belgrade, Zagreb, Warsaw

1957					
Jul	Titus Andronicus	Titus	William Shakespeare	Peter Brook	Stoll
Sep	The Entertainer	Archie Rice	John Osborne	Tony Richardson	Palace
1958					
Feb	The Entertainer	Archie Rice	John Osborne	Tony Richardson	Royale, New York
1959					
Jul	Coriolanus	Coriolanus	William Shakespeare	Peter Hall	Memorial, Stratford-upon-Avon
1960					
Apr	Rhinoceros	Berenger	Eugene Ionesco translated by Derek Prouse	Orson Welles	Royal Court
Jul	Rhinoceros	Berenger	Eugene Ionesco translated by Derek Prouse	Orson Welles	Strand
Oct	Becket	Becket	Jean Anouilh translated by Lucienne Hill	Peter Glenville	St James's, New York
1961					
Mar	Becket	Henry II	Jean Anouilh translated by Lucienne Hill	Peter Glenville	Hudson, New York
1962					
Jul	The Broken Heart	Prologue and Bassanes	John Ford	Laurence Olivier	Chichester Festival
Jul	Uncle Vanya	Astrov	Anton Chekhov translated by Constance Garnett	Laurence Olivier	Chichester Festival
Dec	Semi-Detached	Fred Midway	David Turner	Tony Richardson	Saville
1963					
Jul	Uncle Vanya	Astrov	Anton Chekhov translated by Constance Garnett	Laurence Olivier	Chichester Festival

National Theatre at the Old Vic   1963-1973

1963					
Nov	Uncle Vanya	Astrov	Anton Chekhov translated by Constance Garnett	Laurence Olivier	
Dec	The Recruiting Officer	Captain Brazen	George Farquhar	William Gaskill	
1964					
Apr	Othello	Othello	William Shakespeare	John Dexter	(also Chichester Festival)
Nov	The Master Builder	Solness	Henrik Ibsen adapted by Emlyn Williams	Peter Wood	
1965					
Oct	Love for Love	Tattle	William Congreve	Peter Wood	
1967					
Feb	The Dance of Death	Edgar	August Strindberg translated by C.D. Locock	Glen Byam Shaw	
Sep	A Flea in her Ear	Plucheux	Georges Feydeau translated by John Mortimer	Jacques Charon	(Canadian tour only)
1969					
Jan	Home and Beauty	A.B. Raham	W. Somerset Maugham	Frank Dunlop	
Jul	Three Sisters	Chebutikin	Anton Chekhov translated by Moura Budberg	Laurence Olivier	

DATE	PLAY	ROLE	WRITER	DIRECTOR	THEATRE
National Theatre at the Old Vic 1963-1973					
1970 Apr	The Merchant of Venice	Shylock	William Shakespeare	Jonathan Miller	(also Cambridge)
1971 Dec	Long Day's Journey Into Night	James Tyrone	Eugene O'Neill	Peter Wood	(also New)
1973 Oct	Saturday, Sunday, Monday	Antonio	Eduardo de Filippo adapted by Keith Waterhouse and Willis Hall	Franco Zeffirelli	
Dec	The Party	John Tagg	Trevor Griffiths	John Dexter	

The company went to Moscow and Berlin with Othello *and* Love for Love *in 1965; to Canada with* Love for Love, The Dance of Death *and* A Flea in her Ear *in 1967; and to Los Angeles with* Three Sisters *and* The Beaux' Stratagem *in 1970.*

Films
(including films made for television)

RELEASE DATE	TITLE (US titles in brackets)	ROLE	DIRECTOR	SCREENPLAY/WRITER
1930	The Temporary Widow	Peter Billie	Gustav Ucicky	Karl Hartl, Walter Reisch and Benn Levy from play, *Hokuspokus,* by Curt Goetz
	Too Many Crooks	The Man	George King	Billie Bristow from story by Basil Roscoe
1931	Potiphar's Wife (Her Strange Desire)	Straker	Maurice Elvery	Edgar Middleton from his play
	Friends and Lovers	Lt Nichols	Victor Schertzinger	Jane Murfin from novel, *The Sphinx has Spoken,* by Maurice de Kobra
	The Yellow Passport (The Yellow Ticket)	Julian Rolphe	Raoul Walsh	Jules Furthman and Guy Bolton from play by Michael Morton
1932	Westward Passage	Nick Allen	Robert Milton	Robert Milton from novel by Margaret Barnes
1933	Perfect Understanding	Nicholas Randall	Cyril Gardner	Michael Powell from story by Miles Malleson
	No Funny Business (The Professional Co-respondents)	Clive Dering	John Stafford and Victor Hanbury	Victor Hanbury and Frank Vosper from story by Dorothy Hope
1935	Moscow Nights (I Stand Condemned)	Captain Ignatoff	Anthony Asquith	Erich Siepmann and Pierre Renoit from novel, *Les Nuits de Moscow*
1936	As You Like It	Orlando	Paul Czinner	R.J. Cullen, J.M. Barrie and Carl Meyer from play by William Shakespeare
	Conquest of the Air	Vincent Lunardi	A. Shaw, J.M. Saunders, A. Esway and Z. Korda	Hugh Gray and Peter Bezencenet from story by John Monk Saunders
1937	Fire Over England	Michael Ingolby	William K. Howard	Clemence Dane and Sergei Nolbandov from novel by A.E.W. Mason
	Twenty-One Days	Larry Durant	Basil Dean	Graham Greene and Basil Dean from play, *The First and the Last,* by John Galsworthy
1938	The Divorce of Lady X	Leslie Logan	Tim Whelan	Ian Dalrymple, Arthur Wimperis and Lajos Biro from play, *Counsel's Opinion*, by Gilbert Wakefield
1939	Q Planes (Clouds Over Europe)	Tony McVane	Tim Whelan	Ian Dalrymple from story by Brock Williams, Jack Whittingham and Arthur Wimperis
	Wuthering Heights	Heathcliff	William Wyler	Ben Hecht and Charles MacArthur from novel by Emily Brontë
1940	Rebecca	Maxim de Winter	Alfred Hitchcock	Robert Sherwood, Joan Harrison, Philip Macdonald and Michael Hagar from novel by Daphne du Maurier
	Pride and Prejudice	Darcy	Robert Z. Leonard	Aldous Huxley and Jane Murfin from novel by Jane Austen

RELEASE DATE	TITLE (US titles in brackets)	ROLE	DIRECTOR	SCREENPLAY/WRITER
1941	Words for Battle	Commentator	Humphrey Jennings	Poems by Milton, Browning, Kipling
	Lady Hamilton (That Hamilton Woman)	Lord Nelson	Alexander Korda	Walter Reisch and R.C. Sherriff
	49th Parallel (The Invaders)	Johnnie, the trapper	Michael Powell	Emeric Pressburger
1943	The Demi-Paradise (Adventure for Two)	Ivan Dimitrievitch Kouznetoff	Anthony Asquith	Anatole de Grunwald
1945	Henry V	Henry	Laurence Olivier	William Shakespeare
1948	Hamlet	Hamlet	Laurence Olivier	William Shakespeare
1951	The Magic Box	PC 94	John Boulting	Eric Ambler
1952	Carrie	George Hurstwood	William Wyler	Ruth and Augustus Goetz from novel, *Sister Carrie*, by Theodore Dreiser
1953	A Queen is Crowned	Narrator (voice only)	Castleton Knight (producer)	Christopher Fry
	The Beggar's Opera	Macheath	Peter Brook	Dennis Cannan from comic opera by John Gay
1955	Richard III	Gloucester	Laurence Olivier	William Shakespeare
1957	The Prince and the Showgirl	Grand Duke	Laurence Olivier	Terence Rattigan from his play, *The Sleeping Prince*
1959	The Devil's Disciple	General Burgoyne	Guy Hamilton	John Dighton and Ronald Kibbee from play by Bernard Shaw
1960	Spartacus	Crassus	Stanley Kubrick	Dalton Trumbo from novel by Howard Fast
	The Entertainer	Archie Rice	Tony Richardson	John Osborne from his play
1961	The Power and the Glory	The Priest	Marc Daniels	Dale Wasserman from novel by Graham Greene
1962	Term of Trial	Graham Weir	Peter Glenville	Peter Glenville from novel by James Barlow
1963	Uncle Vanya	Astrov	Laurence Olivier	Moura Budberg from play by Anton Chekhov
1965	Bunny Lake Is Missing	Inspector Newhouse	Otto Preminger	John and Penelope Mortimer from novel by Evelyn Piper
	Othello*	Othello	Stuart Burge	William Shakespeare
1966	Khartoum	The Mahdi	Basil Dearden	Robert Ardrey
1968	Romeo and Juliet	Prologue and Epilogue (voice only)	Franco Zeffirelli	Franco Brusati and Masolino D'Amican from play by William Shakespeare
	The Shoes of the Fisherman	Premier Kamenev	Michael Anderson	Morris West from his novel
1969	Oh! What a Lovely War	Field Marshal Sir John French	Richard Attenborough	From Joan Littlewood stage production based on *The Long Long Trail* by Charles Chilton
	The Battle of Britain	Air Chief Marshal Sir Hugh Dowding	Guy Hamilton	James Kennaway and S. Benjamin Fisz
	The Dance of Death	Edgar	David Giles	C. Locock from play by August Strindberg
	David Copperfield	Creakle	Delbert Mann	Jack Pulman from novel by Charles Dickens
1970	Three Sisters*	Chebutikin	Laurence Olivier	Moura Budberg from play by Anton Chekhov
1971	Nicholas and Alexandra	Count Witte	Franklin J. Schaffner	James Goldman from book by Robert K. Massie
1972	Lady Caroline Lamb	The Duke of Wellington	Robert Bolt	Robert Bolt
	Sleuth	Andrew Wyke	Joseph L. Mankiewicz	Anthony Shaffer from his play
1975	Love Among the Ruins	Sir Arthur Granville-Jones	George Cukor	James Costigan from novel by Angela Thirkell
1976	The Seven-Per-Cent Solution	Moriarty	Herbert Ross	Nicholas Meyer from his novel
	Marathon Man	Dr Christian Szell	John Schlesinger	William Goldman from his novel
1977	Jesus of Nazareth	Nicodemus	Franco Zeffirelli	Anthony Burgess, Suso Cecchi D'Amico and Franco Zeffirelli
	A Bridge Too Far	Dr Spaander	Richard Attenborough	William Goldman from novel by Cornelius Ryan
1978	The Betsy	Loren Hardemann, Sr	Daniel Petrie	William Bast and Walter Bernstein from novel by Harold Robbins
	The Boys From Brazil	Ezra Lieberman	Franklin J. Schaffner	Kenneth Ross and Heywood Gould from novel by Ira Levin
1979	A Little Romance	Julius	George Roy Hill	Allan Burns from novel, *E=MC², Mon Amour*, by Patrick Cavvin

Release Date	Title (US titles in brackets)	Role	Director	Screenplay/Writer
1979	Dracula	Professor Van Helsing	John Badham	W.D. Richter from stage play by Hamilton Deane and John L. Balderstone, from novel by Bram Stoker
1980	The Jazz Singer	Cantor Rabinovitch	Richard Fleischer	Stephen H. Foreman
1981	Clash of the Titans	Zeus	Desmond David	Beverley Cross
1984	The Bounty	Admiral Hood	Roger Donaldson	Robert Bolt from novel *Captain Bligh and Mr Christian* by Richard Hough
	The Last Days of Pompeii	Gaius	Peter Hunt	Carmen Culver from novel by Bulwer Lytton
1985	Wagner	Sandor Lukacs	Tony Palmer	Charles Wood
	The Jigsaw Man	Admiral Sir Gerald Scaith	Terence Young	Jo Eisinger from novel by Dorothea Bennett
	Wild Geese II	Rudolph Hess	Peter Hunt	Reginald Rose from novel, *The Square Circle*, by Daniel Carney
	Peter the Great	King William III	Marvin Chomsky	Edward Anhalt from book by Robert Massie
Unreleased	Inchon	General Douglas MacArthur	Terence Young	Robin Moore

* Films based on National Theatre productions

.

Television

Date	Title	Role	Writer	Director	Company
1937	Macbeth (excerpts)	Macbeth	William Shakespeare	George More O'Ferrall	BBC
1958	John Gabriel Borkman	Borkman	Henrik Ibsen	Christopher Morahan	ATV
1959	The Moon and Sixpence	Charles Strickland	W. Somerset Maugham	Robert Mulligan	NBC
1967	Theatre Royal (charity performance)	Prologue	Cecil Day Lewis	Grahame Turner	Rediffusion
1969	Male of the Species	Host/Narrator	Alun Owen	Charles Jarrott	NBC
1972	Long Day's Journey Into Night	James Tyrone	Eugene O'Neill	Peter Wood	ATV[+]
1973	The Merchant of Venice	Shylock	William Shakespeare	Jonathan Miller	ATV[+]
1974	World at War	Narrator		Jeremy Isaacs (producer)	Thames
1976	The Collection	Harry Kane	Harold Pinter	Michael Apted	Granada*
	Cat on a Hot Tin Roof	Big Daddy	Tennessee Williams	Robert Moore	Granada*
1978	Come Back, Little Sheba	Doc Delaney	William Inge	Silvio Narizzano	Granada*
	Daphne Laureola	Sir Joseph Pitts	James Bridie	Waris Hussein	Granada*
	Saturday, Sunday, Monday	Antonio	Eduardo de Filippo	Allan Bridges	Granada*
1981	Brideshead Revisited	Lord Marchmain	Evelyn Waugh	Charles Sturridge and Michael Lindsay-Hogg	Granada
1982	A Voyage Round My Father	Clifford Mortimer	John Mortimer	Alvin Rakoff	Thames
1983	King Lear	Lear	William Shakespeare	Michael Elliott	Granada
	A Talent for Murder	Dr Wainwright	Jerome Choderov and Norman Panama	Alvin Rakoff	BBC
1984	Mr Halpern and Mr Johnson	Mr Halpern	Lionel Goldstein	Alvin Rakoff	HTV
	The Ebony Tower	Henry Breasley	John Fowles	Robert Knights	Granada

In 1972 Olivier made a series of commercials for Polaroid (seen only in the United States)

[+]National Theatre productions
* Laurence Olivier was producer of the series, *The Best Play of 19-*

Director

DATE	PRODUCTION	AUTHOR	THEATRE
1935	Golden Arrow*	Sylvia Thompson and Victor Cunard	Whitehall
1936	Bees on the Boatdeck*+	J.B. Priestley	Lyric
1945	Henry V (film)*	William Shakespeare	
	The Skin of Our Teeth	Thornton Wilder	Phoenix
1946	King Lear*	William Shakespeare	New
1947	Born Yesterday	Garson Kanin	Garrick
1948	Hamlet (film)*	William Shakespeare	

Old Vic Company on a tour of Australia and New Zealand   1948

1948	The School for Scandal*	Richard Brinsley Sheridan	
	The Skin of Our Teeth*	Thornton Wilder	

Old Vic Company at the New Theatre   1949

1949	The School for Scandal*	Richard Brinsley Sheridan	
	The Proposal	Anton Chekhov translated by Constance Garnett	
	Antigone*	Jean Anouilh translated by Lewis Galantière	

1949	A Streetcar Named Desire	Tennessee Williams	Aldwych
1950	The Damascus Blade	Bridget Boland	Theatre Royal, Brighton and tour
	Venus Observed*	Christopher Fry	St James's
	Captain Carvallo	Dennis Cannan	St James's
1952	Venus Observed	Christopher Fry	Century, New York
1953	The Sleeping Prince*	Terence Rattigan	Phoenix
1955	Richard III (film)*	William Shakespeare	
1957	The Prince and the Showgirl (film)*	Terence Rattigan	
1960	The Tumbler	Benn Levy	Helen Hayes, New York
1962	The Chances	John Fletcher	Chichester Festival
	The Broken Heart*	John Ford	Chichester Festival
1962/3	Uncle Vanya*	Anton Chekhov translated by Constance Garnett	Chichester Festival

National Theatre at the Old Vic   1963-74

1963	Hamlet	William Shakespeare	
	Uncle Vanya*	Anton Chekhov translated by Constance Garnett	
	Uncle Vanya (film)*	Anton Chekhov translated by Constance Garnett	
1965	The Crucible	Arthur Miller	
1966	Juno and the Paycock	Sean O'Casey	
1967	Three Sisters*	Anton Chekhov translated by Moura Budberg	
1968	The Advertisement+	Natalia Ginzburg translated by Henry Reed	
	Love's Labour's Lost	William Shakespeare	
1970	Three Sisters (film)*	Anton Chekhov translated by Moura Budberg	
1971	Amphitryon 38	Jean Giraudoux translated by S.N. Behrman and Roger Gellert	NT at New Theatre
1974	Eden End	J.B. Priestley	

1976	Hindle Wakes (TV)	Stanley Houghton	
1980	Filumena	Eduardo de Filippo adapted by Keith Waterhouse and Willis Hall	St James's, New York

* In all these productions Laurence Olivier appeared
+ Bees on the Boatdeck co-directed with Ralph Richardson
+ The Advertisement co-directed with Donald Mackechnie

Management

Laurence Olivier presented the following productions

Date	Production	Author	Theatre
1935	Golden Arrow	Sylvia Thompson and Victor Cunard	Whitehall
1936	Bees on the Boatdeck*	J.B. Priestley	Lyric
1945	The Skin of Our Teeth	Thornton Wilder	Phoenix
1947	Born Yesterday	Garson Kanin	Garrick
1949	Daphne Laureola	James Bridie	Wyndham's
	Fading Mansions	Jean Anouilh translated by Donagh McDonagh	Duchess
	A Streetcar Named Desire	Tennessee Williams	Aldwych
1950	The Damascus Blade	Bridget Boland	Theatre Royal, Brighton and tour
	Venus Observed	Christopher Fry	St James's
	Captain Carvallo	Dennis Cannan	St James's
	Top of the Ladder	Tyrone Guthrie	St James's
1951	Caesar and Cleopatra	Bernard Shaw	St James's
	Antony and Cleopatra	William Shakespeare	St James's
	The Consul (opera)	Gian Carlo Menotti	Cambridge
	Othello (Orson Welles)	William Shakespeare	St James's
1952	The Happy Time*	Samuel Taylor	St James's
1953	Anastasia	Marcelle Maurette translated by Guy Bolton	St James's
1954	Waiting for Gillian	Ronald Millar	St James's
1956	Double Image	Roger MacDougall and Ted Allan	Savoy
1957	Summer of the Seventeenth Doll	Ray Lawler	New
1959	The Shifting Heart	Richard Beynon	Duke of York's
	One More River	Beverley Cross	Duke of York's
1960	A Lodging for the Bride*	Patrick Kirwan	Westminster
	Over the Bridge*	Sam Thompson	Westminster

Laurence Olivier took over the lease of the St James's Theatre in 1949. The theatre, despite a campaign by the profession, was demolished in 1957 to make way for an office block.

* co-productions

Radio

1935	Jan	The Winter's Tale	1947	Dec	Men of Good Will	1971	Jan	We'll Hear a Play
1941	Apr	For Us The Living	1952	May	A Man I Should Like To Meet (interview)		Oct	Remembering Michel Saint-Denis
1942	Apr	Henry V	1953	Feb	40 Years of Rep (interview)	1972	Apr	Dame Gladys Cooper: A Family Portrait
	Jul	Poetry Reading		Jun	The Beggar's Opera (extract)		Nov	Bound To Let On
	Oct	Christopher Columbus	1954	Jun	Henry VIII	1973	Aug	The Bob Hope Story
	Oct	Maud	1955	Sep	Charter in the Saucer	1976	Feb	Rattigan's Theatre
	Oct	Trafalgar Day	1963	Dec	People Today: Laurence Olivier	1977	Jan	Portrait of Sir William Walton
	Nov	Poems by John Pudney	1964	Nov	Voice of the North (interview)			
	Dec	The School for Scandal	1965	Jul	Interview on the National Theatre			
1943	Dec	Poetry Reading	1966	Apr	Portrait of George Devine			
1944	Feb	The Ancient Mariner		Aug	The Time of My Life: Dame Sybil Thorndike			
1945	Apr	Henry IV Parts I and II	1969	Oct	Sir Laurence Olivier Conversation	(These are all BBC radio productions)		

Awards and Honours

Date	Awards and Honours	Production
1939	Oscar nomination	Wuthering Heights
1940	Oscar nomination	Rebecca
1944	Appointed director of the Old Vic Company	

1946	Oscar: Best Actor
	  also special Oscar for his outstanding
	  achievement as actor, producer and director
	  in bringing *Henry V* to the screen
		Henry V

	Oscar nomination	Hamlet
	MA Hons. Tufts University, Mass	
1947	Knighthood	
1948	Oscars: Best Picture, Best Actor	Hamlet
	British Film Academy Award: Best Film	Hamlet
	Venice Film Festival Award: Best Film	Hamlet
1949	Commander, Order Dannenbrog	
	Officier Légion d'Honneur	
1953	Grande Ufficiale dell'Ordino al Merito della Repubblica (Italian)	

1955	British Film Academy Awards:
	  Best British Film
	  Best Performance by British actor
	  Best Film from any source
		Richard III

1956	Berlin Film Festival Silver Bear Award (second prize for film)	Richard III
	Oscar nomination for Best Actor	Richard III
	Elected President of the Actors' Charitable Trust	
	Selznick Golden Laurel Trophy for contribution to international goodwill	
1957	Hon. D.Litt. Oxon	
	Evening Standard Drama Award	The Entertainer
1959	Emmy	The Moon and Sixpence
1960	Karlovy Vary Film Festival Award	The Entertainer
	Oscar nomination	The Entertainer
1961	Appointed director of the Chichester Festival Theatre	
1962	Appointed director of the National Theatre	
	Cork Film Festival Award	Term of Trial
	Mask of Tragedy (Olympus) Award at the Taormina Film Festival	Term of Trial
1964	Hon. LL D Edinburgh	
1965	Oscar nomination	Othello
1966	Sonning Prize, Denmark	
1967	Evening Standard Drama Award	The Dance of Death
	Plays and Players Award	The Dance of Death
1968	Hon. D.Litt. Manchester	
	Hon. D.Litt. London	

	Gold Medallion Swedish Academy of
	  Literature for his outstanding
	  interpretation of Swedish drama
		The Dance of Death

1969	Society of Film and Television Arts Award	Oh! What A Lovely War
1970	Plays and Players Award	The Merchant of Venice
	Created Life Peer: Baron Olivier of Brighton	
1971	Order of Yugoslavia, Flag with Golden Wreath	
1972	Evening Standard Drama Award	Long Day's Journey Into Night
	Plays and Players Award	Long Day's Journey Into Night

DATE	AWARDS AND HONOURS	PRODUCTION
1973	Emmy	Long Day's Journey Into Night
	New York Film Critics Award	Lady Caroline Lamb
	Oscar nomination	Sleuth
	Evening Standard special award for directorship of the National Theatre	
1974	Emmy	Love Among the Ruins
	Created a Fellow of BAFTA	
1976	Albert Medal, RSA	
1977	Emmy	The Collection
	Variety Club of Great Britain Award	Marathon Man
	Oscar nomination	Marathon Man
1978	Filmex Award	A Little Romance
	Hon. D.Litt. Sussex	
1979	Awarded a special Oscar for 'his unique achievement . . . and for a lifetime contribution to the art of film'	
1981	Order of Merit	
1982	Hollywood Golden Globe Award: Cecil B. de Mille Award for his outstanding contribution to the entertainment field	
	Emmy	Brideshead Revisited
1984	Emmy	King Lear
	The Society of West End Theatre Awards named after Laurence Olivier	

All film and stage awards and nominations are for acting unless otherwise stated

Oscar: awarded by the Academy of Motion Picture Arts and Sciences
Emmy: awarded by the American Academy of Television Arts and Sciences

Plays and Players Award is awarded on the voting of the London Theatre Critics

Index

(Numbers in roman refer to plate captions; numbers in *italic* refer to pages)

Acknowledgments

(Numbers in roman refer to plate captions; numbers in *italic* refer to pages)

The author and the publisher would like to express their appreciation to the following for their assistance and/or permission to reproduce the photographs. Every effort has been made to trace copyright owners and the author and the publisher would like to apologise to anyone whose copyright has unwittingly been infringed.

ATV Network Ltd 139, 141, 142; BB Productions 168; BBC Copyright Photographs 163; BBC Hulton Picture Library: Prologue half title, 1920s half title, 27, 35, 38, 85; Birmingham Repertory Theatre 6, 7, 8, 10, 12, 13, 14, 15, 16, 17, 21; British Home Entertainment Plc: 1960s half title, 118, 125; Cinegate 62; Columbia Pictures Corporation 144; Crawford Films Ltd *10*, 98, 99, 100, 109, 110; Anthony Crickmay 136; Zoë Dominic *13*, 124, 127, 128, 137, 140; John Freebairn-Smith 1; Samuel Goldwyn 61; Granada Television: 1980s half title, 147, 148, 152, 153, 155, 160, 162, 166; HTV Limited 164; Julie Hamilton 101; Harris Films Ltd 30; John Haynes 143; Angus McBean Photograph, Harvard Theater Collection: 1950s half title, 86, 87, 88, 92, 93, 94, 95, 96, 97, 104, 105, 115, 116, 120, 121, 122, 123; ITC Entertainment Limited: 1970s half title, 103, 149, 154; Illustrated London News Picture Library 24; Dino de Laurentiis 165; London Films International Limited 46, 55, 59, 65; London Trust Cultural Productions Ltd 167; LOP Limited 102; Lorimar Productions 151; Metro Goldwyn Mayer/United Artists Entertainment Co 64, 106, 126, 129, 131, 150, 159; Lewis Morley 119; National Film Archives *10, 14*, 1960s half title, 25, 26, 29, 30, 31, 32, 44, 46, 49, 55, 59, 61, 62, 64, 65, 66, 67, 72, 73, 81, 82, 89, 90, 91, 98, 99, 100, 102, 106, 107, 109, 110, 113, 114, 125, 126, 129, 130, 131, 132, 134, 135, 138, 144, 145, 146, 150, 151, 156, 157, 158, 159; The Billy Rose Theatre Collection, The New York Public Library at Lincoln Center: Astor, Lenox and Tilden Foundations: (White Studio) 23, (Vandamm) 34, (Vandamm) 60, (Vandamm) 63, (Joseph Abeles Collection) 111, (Joseph Abeles Collection) 112; Collection Lord Olivier 5, 9, 11; Omnibus Productions 134; Paramount Pictures 90, 113, 130, 132, 146; Pendennis Films Ltd 49; By courtesy of The Rank Organisation Plc *14*, 26, 44, 54, 66, 67, 72, 73, 81, 82; Governors of the Royal Shakespeare Theatre 2; St Edward's School, Oxford 3, 4; Bern Schwartz 6; David Sim 117; Sun Film 32; Gloria Swanson Pictures Corporation Ltd 31; Thames Television Limited 161; Theatre Museum, London: 1930s half title, 18, 19, 20, 22, 28, 36, 41, 42, 43, 50, 52, 53, 57; Thorn EMI Screen Entertainment Ltd 29, 89, 91, 135, 138, 158, 169; John Timbers 108; The Times Newspapers Limited 33, 37, 39, 45; Universal Pictures Ltd 107, 145, 157; Universum Film Aktiengesellschaft 25; John Vickers Archives: Frontispiece, 1940s half title, 68, 69, 70, 71, 74, 75, 76, 77, 78, 79, 80, 83, 84; Victoria and Albert Museum, copyright reserved 40, 47, 48, 51, 56, 58; Warner Bros 114, 156; Reg Wilson 133

The author would like to add a personal note of thanks to: Anita Appel, Jane Birkett, Laurence Bernes, Margaret Duerden, Peter Hirst, Shirley Luke, Don Mead, Andrew Rasanen, Peter Seward, Dorothy L. Swerdlove, Jack Tate, everybody at the Theatre Museum and everybody at the BFI Stills Library.